Sen

Do you know
things you can
Elizabeth Gu
than a hundred offers which will be of special interest to children of all ages. Ranging from records to recipes, maps to models and kits to club membership, they include something for everyone. Lots of the items are free and the rest cheap enough to be bought with your pocket money.

Elizabeth Gundrey lives in London and has written a number of books for children on crafts and activities. She is the author of *All Your Own*, also published by Beavers.

SEND OFF FOR IT

Elizabeth Gundrey

POST OFFICE

Nº1

Beaver Books

First published in 1978 by
The Hamlyn Publishing Group Limited
London · New York · Sydney · Toronto
Astronaut House, Feltham, Middlesex, England
Revised edition published 1979

ISBN 0 600 20038 8

Set, printed and bound by
Cox & Wyman Limited, Reading
Set in Monotype Plantin Light

The publishers are grateful to all the manufacturers who gave permission for us to reproduce or use for reference purposes illustrative material which is their copyright.

INTRODUCTION

'Anything in the post for me?'

'YES!' will be the answer if you make use of this book.

It's full of goodies – some of them free – which you can send for. When you write off for them, check these five things before you post your letter:

1 Have you put your name and address in, clearly written?
2 Have you said exactly what you want sent?
3 Have you enclosed stamps or a postal order for the right amount?
4 Have you copied out the supplier's address correctly?
5 Have you stamped the envelope?

A list at the end of the book tells you how much money to send and where to send it. As you will see, some suppliers ask you to send not just the price of the goods but also the cost of the postage and packing. Occasionally, this may be more than the price of the goods themselves – for example, posters are often rolled up, not folded, and packed in a heavy cardboard tube to protect them. (Such tubes are useful for model-making, by the way.) Often postage for two items ordered at the same time is less than for the two ordered separately – you can ask about this.

The prices stated in the list at the back are correct at the time of writing this book, but if you send for things months or years later, the supplier may tell you that the price has since gone up a bit.

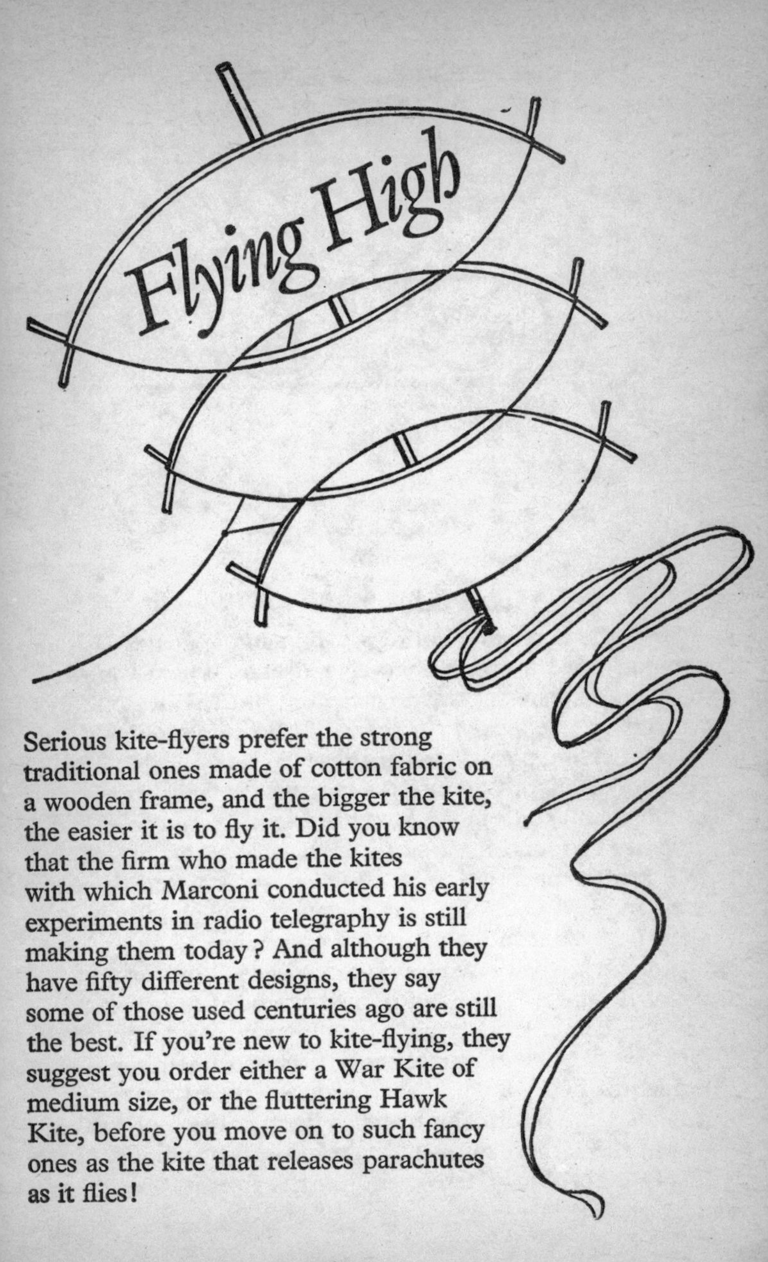

Flying High

Serious kite-flyers prefer the strong traditional ones made of cotton fabric on a wooden frame, and the bigger the kite, the easier it is to fly it. Did you know that the firm who made the kites with which Marconi conducted his early experiments in radio telegraphy is still making them today? And although they have fifty different designs, they say some of those used centuries ago are still the best. If you're new to kite-flying, they suggest you order either a War Kite of medium size, or the fluttering Hawk Kite, before you move on to such fancy ones as the kite that releases parachutes as it flies!

Trams Trains & Trinkets

One of the best day's outings in England is at Beamish – the north of England's open-air museum. There you can ride on old trams or watch ancient steam-engines puff by (including a replica of Stephenson's 'Locomotion' of 1825), explore a small colliery that has been reconstructed, or pop into the cottages or farm buildings of long ago. You can see how historic machines from old factories or foundries used to work, walk across antique iron bridges or into a bygone railway station, and there's even an old schoolroom (complete with the children's slates), a bandstand, a pharmacy and a signal box.

Too far to visit? Well, you can still send off for a little bit of Beamish. Those old trams have been turned into cut-and-colour models and a small jigsaw. And, for any girl who likes charm bracelets but wants something a bit different, there's a gilt chain necklace with a tiny gilt miner's lamp on it. The Beamish T-shirt has a picture of one of the earliest rail-trucks used to carry coal. There are lots of other things, too – send for the free list.

New hobbies

The toy people, Galts, are also a good source of fresh ideas on crafts – and not just ideas: they supply the materials too. The ones they find most popular at present are these:

Paper-making Using pulp, size, moulds, gauze, a special pulper and some colouring, you can produce sheets of writing-paper with envelopes to match. All you need supply yourself is old newspapers.
Fabric collage This kit supplies materials and cutting-out shapes to make a gay picture. You need scissors and glue.
Instant papier-maché None of the bother usually involved in shredding and boiling newspapers: the tub of papery stuff plus adhesive makes a fine, hard modelling material for masks, figures and so forth. Enough to make heads for forty puppets, for instance.
New-clay This is better than ordinary clay because it contains nylon, which means your models won't be brittle when they have dried. They can be painted.
Fun with Art This is a book with dozens of ideas for making pictures without drawing, for example prints, wax, bleach, ink-blots and tissue collage.

Don't forget!

1 Write your name and address clearly and say exactly what you want

2 Send the correct money in stamps or postal orders (not cash)

3 Enclose a big enough stamped addressed envelope, if required

4 Address your envelope correctly and stamp it

Finding out what's where

'History is about chaps, geography is about maps,' somebody once said. But not all maps are about geography, as a famous map-making company have realised. Bartholomew's FREE catalogue is full of pictorial maps dealing with subjects as varied as postage stamps, railways and their history, Bonnie Prince Charlie, the Armada, Scottish clans and tartans, the Queen's ancestors, the world's flowers, animals, birds, insects, vintage cars, football history, Drake's voyages in the *Golden Hinde*, famous scientists and inventors, coins of Europe, horses, planes and ships. Take your pick!

All these maps are big, colourful, and packed with pictures and information – they'd make a colourful splash on your wall, but are full of interest even if kept folded up among your books.

Holidays with a difference

Have you ever thought of having an outdoor holiday, full of sports and other lively activities? Or of spending your holiday pursuing your favourite hobby somewhere – or learning a new one?

If any of these ideas appeal to you, you can find out what's available by getting a useful guide published by the English Tourist Board.

'Activity and Hobby Holidays in England '79' is for all the family if they're keen on activities from archery to surfing, ballooning to pot-holing, fencing to fishing.

The guide also gives details of all kinds of hobbies and holiday-places that provide for them – things like archaeological digs, arts and crafts, birdwatching, drama, music and lots else.

FREE!

FOOT GAMES

Clarks, the shoe people, have a little book of games to play with your toes and feet. They've worked them out because wiggling your toes and stretching your feet makes them straighter, stronger and healthier. If you'd like to have a go, and also learn a little bit about how to tell whether your shoes are a good fit, write for 'Fun for 10 Toes' to this address:

Clarks, Street, Somerset.

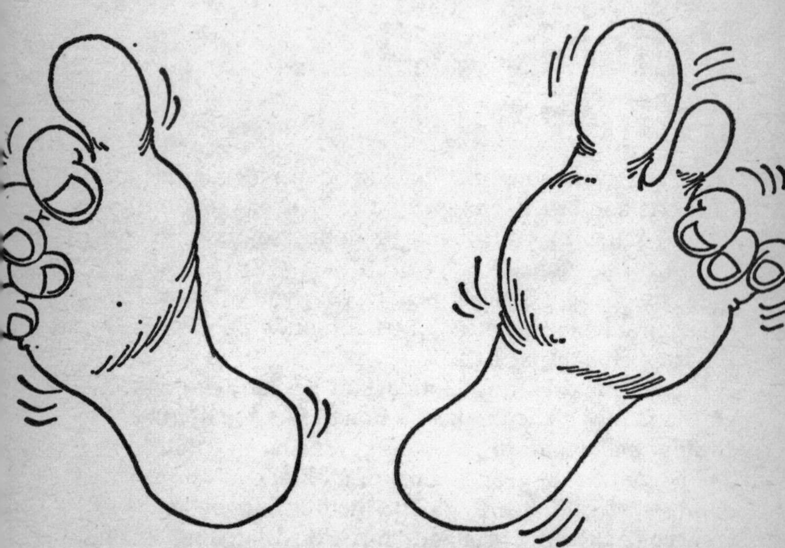

Wildlife posters

Print of front paw

Museums are great places for finding posters of very good quality, often at very low prices. For example, the Natural History Museum in London has a big selection and a free catalogue that illustrates them all in colour (well worth getting). Some favourites are:

a series of fifteen posters showing the different plants of meadows, hedgerows, woodlands, etc., with really beautiful colour drawings by Barbara Nicholson;

Chi-Chi the Panda (this one is particularly good value);

and a chart of British butterflies.

Smaller but very beautiful are the Museum's colour prints – including some lovely ones of woodpeckers, an owl and moths. All these are by artists of the 18th or 19th centuries.

Young volunteers

If you want to enjoy your next school holidays doing something different, meeting people and discovering more about yourself, try a little voluntary work.

It might be with playgroups or handicapped children, working on a farm or an archaeological dig, or helping in a hospital or with a conservation project; it might be near your home or far away (even abroad). Choose which you prefer. If you don't want vigorous physical work, there are plenty of less strenuous openings.

To get an idea of what's available, you can write off for the latest issue of the Voluntary Service Opportunities Register. Most of the openings are for over-sixteens but some are suitable for over-thirteens.

The real Red Indians

One of the hunting tribes of the Canadian Arctic was the Naskapi, who lived on the caribou of Labrador. They hunted these animals not only for their meat but for their hides, from which they made clothes and covers for their lodges (tents). From the bones and antlers they made tools, the stringy sinews were used for thread, and they made bags out of the stomachs of the caribou. The Naskapi used to wait by the rivers where the herds crossed during their migration each year, slaughtering as many as they could to store for use during the icy winter.

The Naskapi loved decorating the hides with red, yellow and blue dyes that they mixed with fish roe. They were fond of curving patterns like the one shown here, easy to apply with a sharpened bit of caribou antler (and easy for you to copy, using fabric paint).

You can get a huge wallchart (125 × 75 cm) showing in large colour photographs the decorated hide clothes of the Naskapi, a ceremonial drum, a pipe and various tools.

The 'Naskapi' wallchart is one of several on North American Indians produced by the Royal Ontario Museum. Others feature 'Toys and Games', 'Musical Instruments', 'Wood Cree', 'Quill Work' and 'Assiniboine'. Each comes with a leaflet printed in English and French because both languages are spoken in Canada.

All about dinosaurs

The place for dinosaurs is, of course, the Natural History Museum in London, with its spectacular collection of fossilised skeletons. Even if you can't visit it, the Museum will gladly send you dinosaurs by the dozen in the shape of models, pictures, books and so on.

First, the models. These are made strictly to scale – $\frac{1}{40}$ of their real size. They're plastic – green, grey, brown or fawn – and their lengths range from 100 to 520 mm.

There are also nine posters with a different dinosaur on each, thirteen colour and several black-and-white postcards. Three dinosaurs are commemorated on badges. The Museum also has a huge wallchart on 'The Age of the Dinosaurs', a wall-plaque featuring Tyrannosaurus and a dinosaur book.

Coming soon are four dinosaur 3-D jigsaws and four poster-leaflets. Write for details.

The Birmingham Museum sells eight colourful postcards of dinosaurs in a plastic wallet, which you could join together to make a frieze 120 cm long, if you liked.

The Roman Wall

One of Britain's most spectacular ruins is the 113-kilometre wall built nearly two thousand years ago, when Britain was a colony of Rome. It stretches right across England from Carlisle to Newcastle, and recently archaeologists have excavated more of the forts and other buildings that can now be visited at different spots along it.

A yellow chart tells the whole story, with lots of drawings, a map and a date list. You can get a very vivid idea of how the Legionaries lived (there's even a Roman lavatory illustrated!), how they were armed, what they wore, the gods they worshipped and the kind of tombstones they carved.

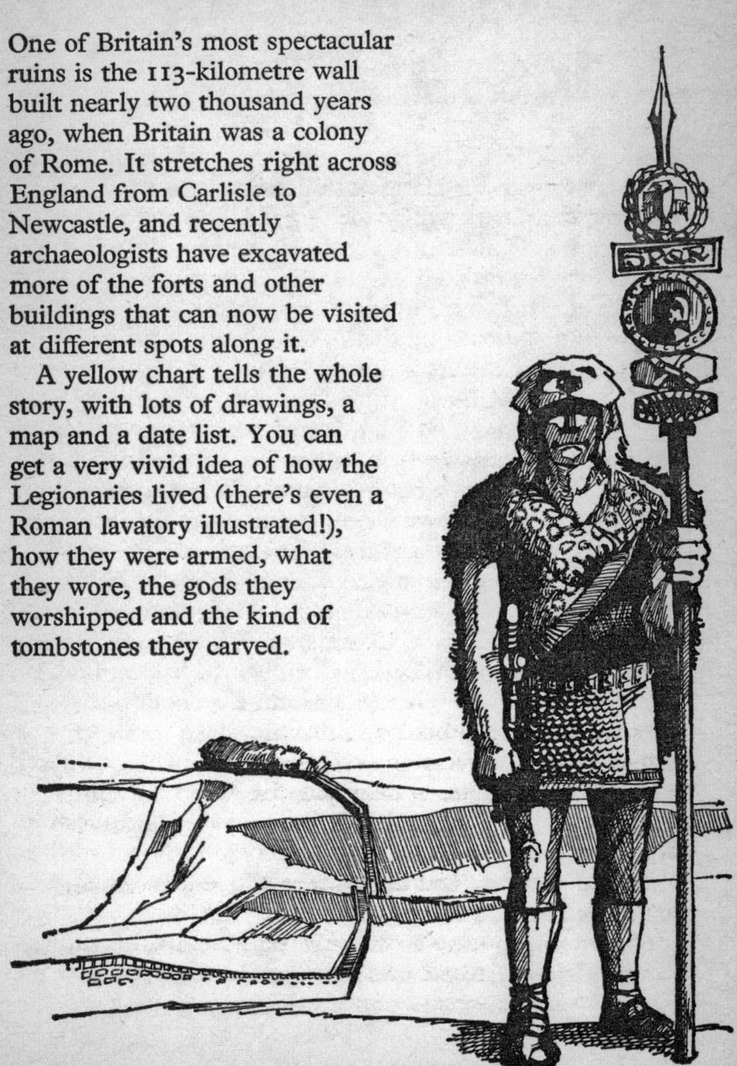

Who's afraid of the big, bad exam?

Beginning to feel a bit nervous as O-Levels loom ahead? One way to take the alarm out of exams is to know exactly what the examiners will be looking for. Did you realise, for instance, that in maths getting the right answer to a problem counts for very little on its own? Higher marks go to those who set out their work in such a way that the examiner can see the line of reasoning that is being followed.

A publisher has come up with the very bright idea of taking a lot of GCE exam questions that have actually been set in the past, and then following each with a model answer – done in just the way the examiners like to see answers written. (How does he know? Because he got some real-life examiners to write down the model answers for the book!)

The following subjects have been covered:

O-Level: English language, English literature, Maths, Physics, Chemistry, Biology, Geography, History, French, Economics, Commerce, West African History and Sociology; A-Level: Chemistry, Physics, Biology, Pure Maths, Applied Maths and Economics.

Another very useful book you may not have come across is called 'Your Choice at 13+'. This is full of advice about exactly which subjects to go in for when making your selection for CSE or GCE. It asks all sorts of questions which will help you decide what kind of job will suit you best when you grow up, and then it tells you which exam passes you'll need in order to get into your chosen career. It's very important not to drop a particular subject at thirteen, only to find it's going to be absolutely essential to you later on.

A trip to the theatre

Did you know that you can join the audience at some of your favourite TV or radio shows? Write to the television (or radio) station concerned and ask what is available. There is generally a waiting-list of several months, so apply well in advance. Mention your age and the type of show you would like to see being recorded. The minimum age limit is 10 for radio shows and 14 for most TV shows.

If you live in or near London, send a stamped addressed envelope with your application to:

The BBC Ticket Unit, Broadcasting House, Portland Place, London W1A 4WW.

Embroidery know-how

How many different kinds of embroidery stitch can you do? How many different kinds do you think there are altogether? Probably no one has counted them all, but there are a hundred in a booklet produced by Coats (the people who manufacture sewing-thread). Very clear diagrams show you how to do each one. The two examples shown here are Blanket Stitch and Sheaf Stitch, both very easy to do. Sheaf Stitch is particularly decorative if you use two contrasting colours.

Even better, though it shows only fifty stitches, is another booklet from the same firm, printed in two colours and giving some imaginative ideas for designs to embroider with each stitch, from owls to apples, sparrows to soldiers.

How to make posters

If you ever get involved in designing posters for school, a club you belong to or anything else, you may like to obtain a leaflet telling you how to make lots of copies by using an organdie screen and printing-ink.

Don't forget!

1 Write your name and address clearly and say exactly what you want

2 Send the correct money in stamps or postal orders (not cash)

3 Enclose a big enough stamped addressed envelope, if required

4 Address your envelope correctly and stamp it

London life in bygone times

The London Museum is perhaps the most fascinating museum in England if you like history. It's in a very modern building, but inside it old shops, transport, homes – even the interior of a Roman villa – have been recreated. Do visit it if you can, but if you can't, send off for the list of fascinating things you can order by post from the museum. You're bound to find something that interests you – coins, pictures, old maps, old photos, mugs, pens, models of old transport, bricks with which to build St Pauls, jigsaws, dolls, model figures, books and slides.

Here are just a few of the unusual things you can buy by post:

'The History of Little Fanny'. This is a replica of a small book (in a box) which was first published about 1830. It tells a sad story in verse about a little girl who is kidnapped (but gets home in the end), and as you turn each page you find a cut-out coloured doll with which to create Fanny in each of her different costumes.

Two board games – one on English history from Roman times to the date when this was first published (1848), and the other on railway adventures (also published about then, not long after the railways first started to spread across Britain). These come on large sheets of thin card, with charming old pictures in colour, together with their rules. You provide your own counters or cut-up cards to move round the board as you play.

The Museum has a lot of Victorian puppets and they have used two of these to make a poster of Punch and Judy in the showman's booth, gaily painted.

Lastly, there are tins big enough to hold half a pound of biscuits, shaped like little houses, each one designed like an old-time shop. There is a baker, a sweet shop, a tea merchant and a coffee merchant.

FREE!

Getting in the swim

How many swimming strokes can you do? Would you know what to do if you were in a boat that sank?

You can get a free leaflet showing how to do front crawl, back stroke and breaststroke. It also has useful tips about survival swimming, for instance the correct way to leap into the water if your boat is going down, and staying afloat even if you can't swim (you can quickly turn trousers or skirt into a buoyancy bag to help you).

The leaflet is sponsored by the Yorkshire Bank in Leeds, and you can get it from:
Amateur Swimming Association, Harold Fern House, Derby Square, Loughborough, Leics.

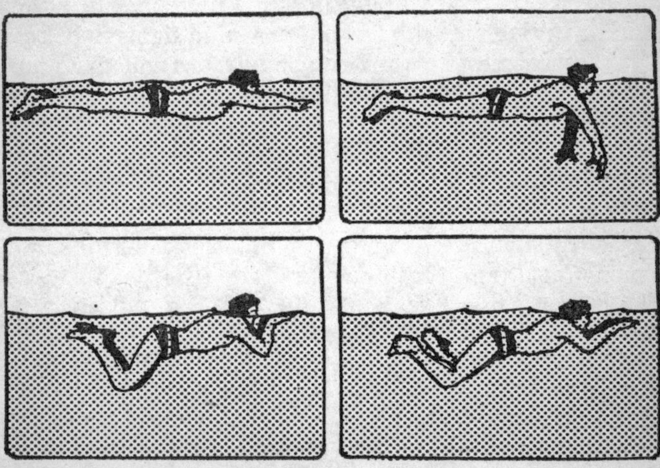

Canals are having a comeback

Much of Britain is criss-crossed by canals that used to be full of heavily-laden boats, drawn along by horses on the tow-paths, until the railways and then the lorries took over. Many canals then became neglected and forgotten until, in fairly recent years, people began to realise what they were missing.

A trip or, better still, a holiday on a canal is full of interest. You're close to the wildlife of the waterside – the birds, fish, water-plants, perhaps even a shy water-vole or shrew. There's the endless fascination of seeing how the locks work, looking at all the different kinds of bridges including aqueducts (huge bridges carrying canals across valleys, with rivers flowing below), drifting through dark tunnels and admiring some of the old 'narrow boats', painted with roses and castles, that still survive. Even if you live in a city, there may be a canal running through it, with lots of interesting sights to be seen.

If you become an enthusiast you can start collecting canal finds and books on the subject. A good source for these is the British Waterways Board, which has premises in London and in Watford and will send things by post. Among some excellent things it offers are posters nearly 60 × 75 cm, each one a superb colour photograph of a canal scene – an aqueduct of the Lancaster Canal, a flight of locks on the Grand Union Canal, and locks on the Caldon Canal. They also have several first-rate books for children – 'Canals are Great', 'Fun on the Waterways' and 'The Story of our Canals'. Of these, the second one is the best to take on a journey because it's full of spotting and recording exercises. The third one is colourful, and concentrates on the history of the canals.

A guide to garden birds

Can you recognise all the birds in your garden, and do you know how to attract more birds to it?

Colourful photographs, plus a text that describes the birds' different habits of feeding, flying or nesting, will help you to tell one from another if you send for this free booklet. It also advises you on what kind of food to put out or plants to grow, and how to make a bird-table and nesting-boxes.

To get the booklet, simply send 19p in stamps for postage to the RSPB, and at the same time ask about joining their Young Ornithologists Club. The address is:

The Royal Society for the Protection of Birds, The Lodge, Sandy, Bedfordshire SG19 2DL

Making music

Gangadar is a musician who pots or a potter who makes music, whichever way you like to look at him. And he makes something really special which you can send for – ocarinas.

Have you ever seen those little pottery birds or animals which whistle or warble when you blow through them ? An ocarina is a musical instrument which works in a similar way, but because it has a lot of holes you can, if your fingers are dextrous and your ear for music keen, play all kinds of tunes on it. The ocarina isn't new – it's an old, old instrument which the natives of South America were playing long before Christopher Columbus discovered that continent.

Gangadar makes them in three sizes, all hanging like a pendant on a cord to wear round your neck. The smallest and most fascinating has a very sweet high-pitched sound and like the others is tuned to a full major scale: such a tiny thing and yet so very musical.

P is for pasta

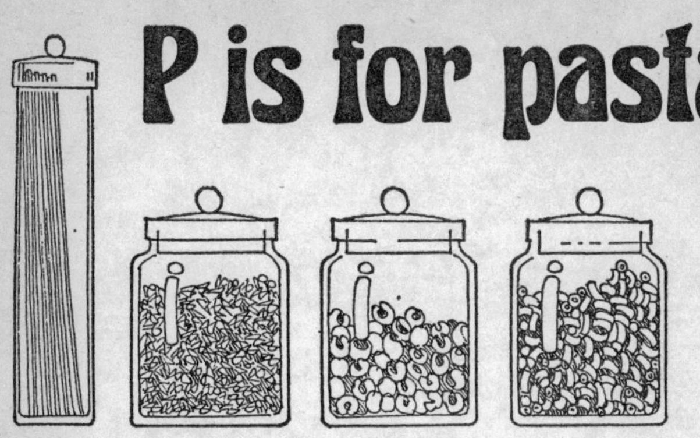

Pasta comes in all kinds of shapes, from alphabet letters to Ziti tagliati, through the more familiar Macaroni, Noodles and Spaghetti – some long, some short, some folded or shaped. Most people connect pasta with Italian dishes such as Spaghetti Bolognese or Ravioli but in fact it was a Chinese invention. If you want to know more about it (including how the hole gets into macaroni) you can buy a brown-and-orange poster with all the answers, or send for a set of FREE leaflets which give lots of recipes among which you'll find some you can make yourself (enclose a stamped addressed envelope at least 25 cm long).

Here's a recipe calculated to fill a dozen hearty 'cowboys' of either sex, if they've the usual 7-to-12-year-old appetite. It's easy to serve and easy to keep warm:

Cowboys' Bean and Pasta Bake

Cook 250 g macaroni rings in boiling salted water until just tender, then drain and stir them into 500 ml white sauce together with at least 50 g grated cheese. Empty a large can of baked beans into a greased oven dish, spread the macaroni over, then top with a second canful of beans. Sprinkle with more grated cheese. (You can do all that well in advance if you like.) Bake for $\frac{1}{2}$ hour (mark 5, or 375°F) before serving.

A pond in your room

Here's a real eye-catcher to adorn your room. It's a slot-together kit, and all you have to do is fold and press the different parts into position, and paint them. When complete you have a three-dimensional model nearly 40 cm high, showing an underwater scene with water weeds and a roach swimming, while up above are bull rushes, an alder tree, sand-martins and a moorhen. Lift a flap and you'll even find a water-rat's tunnel.

With the kit comes a leaflet telling you about pond life, and other items which you can slot in as and when you like – insects, kingcups, newt, dragonfly, kingfisher and so on. Visit a local pond and you'll soon spot other plants and creatures to add to your own.

The same firm produces models of castles, a doll's house and a vintage car – ask for their free leaflet if you're interested.

MAKE or 'BREAK

That's the name of a kit you can use either to repair broken china and suchlike, or to make little models and things like beads, paperweights, cufflinks, earrings or a china-like nameplate to screw on your door.

In the kit is a special putty: it comes in two parts and, once these are mixed, it begins to set rock-hard. This is what you use to fill in chips or missing bits on things like china figures or mugs, or to model ornaments yourself. There's also a very powerful glue (this, too, is in two parts needing to be mixed), so that you can stick china to china or to putty. A craft knife helps the work along, and there is a paintbrush too – used for the six colours and for the glaze with which you decorate your finished work. A little bottle of thinner is provided for cleaning the brush. There are even some Zodiac and flower designs included, which you can cut out and use as stencils if you are short of ideas for patterns of your own, and, of course, a good instruction book. The whole kit is neatly packed in a pull-out drawer.

Something for eggheads

'All About Eggs' is the name of a full-colour leaflet for young readers which is given away by the British Egg Information Service. It is designed so that it can be made into two posters, and is full of information about the main methods of egg production, marketing, the work of packing stations and the Eggs Authority, and ways in which eggs are used for manufacturing purposes. It tells you all about the nutritional value of eggs, and gives you some easy recipes as well as ideas about what you can do with eggs apart from eating them, like blowing and then decorating them to hang up. The whole secret of blowing is to pierce both ends of the egg first with a needle and then a skewer, making sure you prick the yolk inside. Holding the egg over a bowl, blow down through the broad end and slowly the egg will drop out of the shell, which you can then paint. Finally thread a cotton through the holes, fastening a bead below, and hang up the egg.

To get your copy of 'All About Eggs', send your address and a stamp to cover postage to:

The British Egg Information Service, 37 Panton Street, London SW1Y 4EW

wild places in your world

What kind of place do you live in? What sort of countryside is nearest to your home?

If it is any of the following, do write for a free, colour-illustrated leaflet telling you about the wildlife to be found there:

Lowland farmland; Sand dunes; Salt marshes; The Last Glaciation (the wildlife of Britain 8,000 years ago).

These excellent leaflets come from the Nature Conservancy Council, a government body which is very worried by the way in which places like these are being altered by man so much that our once beautiful countryside is being spoiled and animals or birds driven out. The Council can send you another leaflet too, about nature conservation, and it can tell you where there are nature reserves that you can visit – places where wildlife is protected from harm.

You can also buy large wallcharts showing the wild animals and plants to be found in many of our wild places (see Index for details).

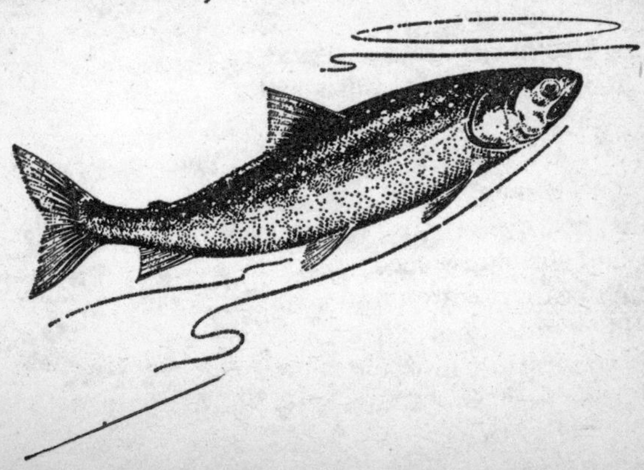

Have you got green fingers?

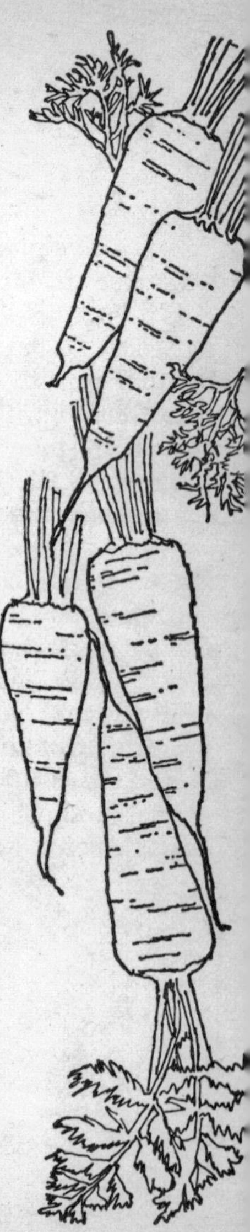

You don't necessarily need a lot of space in order to try your hand as a gardener, for many flowers and even vegetables do well in pots or window boxes. What you *do* need, for most things, is sunshine. Also enough patience (and memory) not to forget to water your plants regularly.

One seed firm, in particular, understands young gardeners and their needs. Suttons have produced special seed collections for children, which can be bought by post. They are good value because if you ordered each item separately you would pay at least 6p more. All carry instructions, of course.

The vegetable collection includes carrot, cress, lettuce, marrow and radishes. The flower collection has marigold, candytuft, clarkia, nasturtium and love-in-a-mist.

They also have a 'mustard-and-cress farm' for indoors. This consists of a plastic tray, absorbent pad, and the two kinds of seeds which grow together. You will soon get many crops, lasting for months, just by damping the pad with water and sprinkling seeds on.

Mung beans are grown in a similar way. They quickly produce the bean-shoots you eat in Chinese restaurants.

Cardboard dolls

A number of museums now sell costume dolls in cardboard. First you cut out the lady in her undies (it's fascinating to see just what did go underneath in past centuries!), then you cut out three or four dresses and hats from her wardrobe in which to clothe her. Most of these card dolls aren't coloured, but are designed for you to paint yourself to your own liking. The dolls are made to stand up. You could assemble quite a collection if you got dolls from a lot of different museums. Here are some to start you off:

Museum of Costume – ladies of 1830, 1860, 1880;
Royal Scottish Museum – in colour. One doll with dresses of 1820–1920.

Creatures great and small

Bees, bats or bears – what's your fancy? If there's any creature you're specially interested in, the chances are that the Natural History Museum in London will have an illustrated leaflet full of interesting information about your favourite. Among the most popular are pandas, earthworms, insects, water-insects, butterflies, whales, penguins, birds of prey and sharks.

The whale leaflet points out that these fish-like creatures are really mammals – warm-blooded, and giving birth to and suckling their young just like other animals do. They have a thick layer of fat, called blubber, to keep them warm even in icy seas. Their big tails power them along by moving up and down (fishes' tails move from side to side) while they steer with their two front flippers. Whales have to keep surfacing to breathe air in, and then hold their breath when they dive – possibly for as long as ¾ hour. When a whale 'spouts' from its nostrils, which are on top of its head, it is not blowing out water but a foam from its lungs which it uses to help when holding its breath. The whale's tiny eyes see very little, but it has a sonar system – it sends out sound waves which echo back to tell the whale when there is some object ahead of it. Only the Killer Whale attacks other mammals (it will even kill the huge Blue Whales, twice its size).

Because of the heavy slaughter of whales, these and some other kinds of whale are almost extinct now.

For busy bees

Anyone who enjoys making things likes to hear of new ideas – or of old ones not yet tried. There are lots of books about crafts, of course, but until you're sure how keen you are you may not want to spend as much money as that.

So it's useful to know where you can get leaflets which, for a few pence, tell you all that you need to know to start up a fresh craft. Answer: Women's Institutes. Although many of their things are for experienced needlewomen or cooks, there are others at which anyone could have a go.

Examples are: 'Knitting for Beginners', 'Basic Macramé' and 'Simple Wood Sculpture'. Then there's 'Broomstick Crochet' – it's different, quick and easy (the loops go round a whizz-pin or broomstick which you grip between your knees while you work). 'Log Cabin Patchwork' builds up patterns from strips of fabric, not the usual hexagons which are more difficult to cut out. 'Collage and Fabric Pictures' and 'Paper Sculpture' are two other good ideas. If you're really neat with your fingers, making 'Embroidered Boxes' might appeal to you, while a delightful leaflet to use after a wintry country walk or car-ride is 'Hedgerow Baskets': gather the kind of twigs recommended and, when they are dry, weave them into big or small baskets (very clear diagrams are given in this and all the other leaflets).

Finally, two small books from the Women's Institutes: 'Soft Toys Galore', and 'Bits for Bazaars' which has fifteen toys and other things you might make for charity or a school fête (though you may be tempted to keep the mittens, moccasins or purse for yourself!)

There are lots more things covered by leaflets – why not send for the complete list (free)?

Pretty plants–with a warning

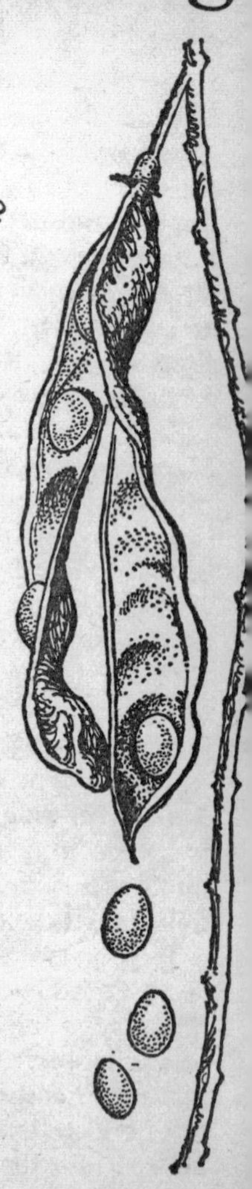

You can't tell by its looks whether a flower or berry is poisonous, but some of the most beautiful ones are the most deadly if eaten. What could be prettier than the red berries of the poisonous yew?

In your garden, beware of lupin seeds, *any* part of the laburnum tree, monkshood (also called aconite), meadow saffron (the autumn crocus) and lily-of-the-valley.

In the countryside or on waste ground, beware of the nightshade – some kinds have white flowers and black berries, some have purple flowers and red berries, and all are risky. Inside the prickly fruit of the thornberry are deadly seeds. The bryony creeper has berries that can kill. Hemlock, easily mistaken for cow parsley, is sometimes picked by children in order to use its hollow stems for peashooters. Don't! Your mouth will be badly burnt, and worse may follow.

And, of course, there are toadstools which can kill. The most sinister is the death-cap, which looks rather like a mushroom; fly agaric is the red one with white dots, which can make you very ill.

If you don't recognise these plants from their names, you need clear coloured pictures of them – and that is exactly what you'll get if you send for a Poisonous Plants Chart to hang on your wall.

A mediæval touch

Salisbury Museum has had a lot of replicas made of old treasures in its collection – things to wear or to display in your room. For instance, there are rings bearing replica coins of Edward the Confessor or Ethelred the Unready, the king who was never prepared when Vikings raided England! Also silver-coloured pendants on chains, including a blue enamelled one with two lions (the original belonged to a 13th century noblewoman, the Countess Ela), and another with a design of the sun and the moon, modelled on the kind of badge pilgrims wore in the 14th century. You can also get a little red brooch made in the shape of a hare, which was originally a Roman enamelled brooch.

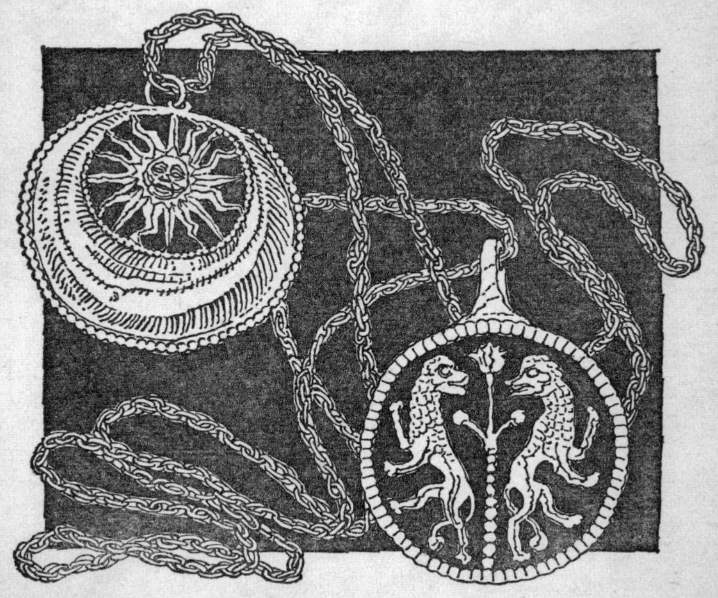

FREE!

Coins and their history

One of the best wallcharts in this book is actually being given away!

It's a huge one telling the story of English coinage in fourteen dramatic colour pictures of incidents in the lives of monarchs and the coins associated with them.

For instance, there's the story of a rather special silver coin that was minted in the time of Queen Anne. We were at war with Spain then, and our forces raided and sacked the port of Vigo. In the harbour were some treasure-ships newly-arrived from South America and full of 'pieces of eight' destined for the Spanish treasury. These were seized, and the silver was brought to England to be melted down and made into English coins stamped with Queen Anne's head and the triumphant word VIGO.

Send a postcard to this address for your chart:

Lloyds Bank Ltd (Public Relations Dept), 71 Lombard Street, London EC3P 3BS

That's the message of a big campaign to put an end to litter in the streets and countryside. Lots of schools and youth clubs are joining in, but every single person can do his or her bit too.

To help things along, the Keep Britain Tidy Group are handing out a lot of things – some free, some not. For instance, you can get as many as twelve transfers FREE (provided you send a 12p stamped large envelope). They are 15 cm square and bright green with 'Keep Britain Tidy' on them together with the campaign symbol shown here. Use them sensibly: dotting them about just anywhere could *add* to the littered look of the streets if you aren't careful.

Why not start a Keep Britain Tidy committee at your school? A free leaflet explains how to do this.

A lot of your favourite personalities have joined the tidy-up campaign, and you can get campaign posters, T-shirts, badges and stickers with them on or with other eye-catching designs. There's a FREE colour leaflet showing the choice. Typical examples are: colour posters with Ronnie Corbett, Lulu, Abba, Donald Duck or the Wombles; white T-shirts with colourful Mickey Mouse or Donald Duck and plain yellow ones with the 'Keep Britain Tidy' slogan (small or medium sizes); badges with Mickey, Donald or the Wombles' slogan. You don't *have* to be a tidy person to qualify for these goodies, but it helps!

One of the best travel booklets being given away comes from the Wales Tourist Board, and it's called simply 'Wales'. It's crammed with pictures and information about the country, some of which perhaps even the Welsh themselves don't know! You'll find hundreds of things to do and places to visit when on holiday there. Write to:

Wales Tourist Board, P.O. Box 151, WDO, Cardiff CF5 1XS

If you're keen on sewing...

Here's something really new if you enjoy needlework and want fresh ideas.

Dewhursts, the sewing-thread people, have produced a series of really attractive kits on different subjects – Patchwork, Cushions, Table Linens and Soft Toys. What exactly do you get? Let's take a look at the Soft Toys kit.

It comes in a large plastic wallet with a pink-and-yellow teddy bear design on the front. Open it up and you find a series of sheets, packets, cards and patterns telling you everything you may want to know – there's even a history of rag dolls included. The first sheet shows what equipment and materials you need to get together, with a list of useful suppliers of things like fur-fabric remnants, glass eyes and stuffings. A colourful folder (well worth stretching out and putting up as a wall frieze) is full of hints on how to make toys – especially details like horses' tails, expressive eyes, cats' whiskers, noses and ears. There are diagrams of all the stitches you may need to use. Packets contain paper patterns for two big toys – a dragon and a hobby horse. Then there are colourful cards with full cutting diagrams and instructions to make a poodle, a tiger, a glove-puppet, a beanbag turtle, a family of rabbits and squirrels, pocket-size dolls, and a whole mini-zoo to hang up. Finally, there's a kangaroo tidy-bag to keep your bits and pieces in.

Everything is so gay you'll long to get started the minute you've opened up your kit. And the other three in the series are just as enticing – the Cushions one is strong on ideas for embroidery and other decorations, the patchwork one (which includes dozens of the cardboard hexagons needed for this work) will use up lots of your fabric scraps if you have enough patience, and the Table Linen one is a good choice if you want to make presents or things to sell at a bazaar.

Something to paint

Two really good colouring books come from London's Natural History Museum. The first ('Natural History Museum Colouring Book') has pictures of all kinds of creatures from butterflies to giraffes (and some interesting information about them, too). If you visit the Museum you can colour the pictures to match the exhibits on show there, otherwise use your own imagination or look them up in books. The second ('What Do Animals Eat ?') describes food-chains and has some marvellous double-page pictures of woodlands and seashores.

For young zoologists

If you're really keen on studying wildlife, the catalogue from Watkins & Doncaster is a 'must' because they supply everything a naturalist could possibly want – books, equipment, even specimens.

For instance, you can get a glass case showing the life history of a ladybird, tortoiseshell butterfly or even a locust, each containing mounted specimens of every stage in the insect's life; or a collection of all the different kinds of fir cones there are, mounted on a board and labelled. There are also big pin-up pictures of insects, shown enlarged to about 45 cm long, in full colour. Then there is a whole range of charts – butterflies, moths, birds (8 charts), mammals (6), fish (4) and trees (4). The last four sets are also produced in miniature, so that you can buy a complete set of these small ones if you prefer this to buying the big charts individually. If you want to try breeding insects, you can get a transparent tube with a removable metal base as well as a special lid which allows the insects to breathe, and there is a beginner's butterfly net. (Remember to release the butterflies or other insects after you have had a close look at them, and maybe made drawings.)

Don't forget!

1 Write your name and address clearly and say exactly what you want

2 Send the correct money in stamps or postal orders (not cash)

3 Enclose a big enough stamped addressed envelope, if required

4 Address your envelope correctly and stamp it

Scotland for Children

That's the title of two chunky books full of puzzles, quizzes and drawing games. Book One has a cut-out model of the Loch Ness monster; Book Two a Round Scotland game.

Fun with colour

You've probably heard of tie-and-dye and batik, but do you know what else you can do with dyes?

Dylon, the dye makers, have free leaflets describing the following things: decorating eggs by dyeing, batik and other methods, colouring flour-and-water dough to model and bake into jewellery or a picture frame, painting designs on clothes with the all-fabric paint, batiking paper for gift-wrapping, and making tie-and-dye fabrics into greetings cards, a toy kitten or a collage. There's also an eight-page introduction to tie-and-dye.

As well as these free items, you can order Dylon kits for tie-and-dye and fabric painting from a shop called Allcraft. The fabric painting kit contains six pots of paint (paints can also be bought individually). Lastly Allcraft sells four transfer packs – Pop Designs, Flowers and Fruit, Zodiac Signs and Letters and Numerals. These are iron-on pictures which you fill in with fabric paints.

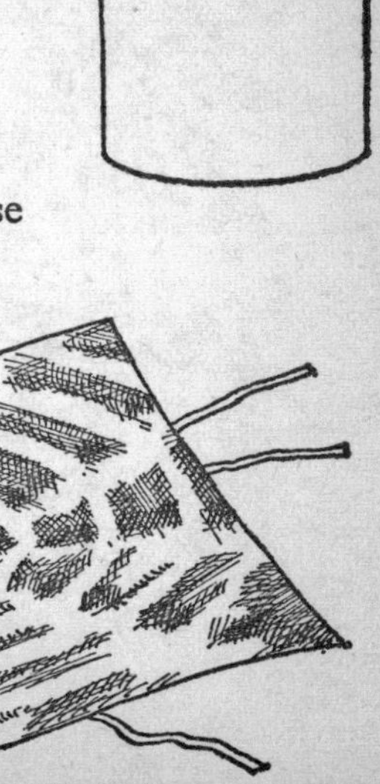

Toy theatres–plus plus plus!

A man called Benjamin Pollock kept on producing a beautiful Victorian toy long after others had stopped. Thanks to him, we can still buy the fantastical, magical little theatres which Robert Louis Stevenson wrote about in *Penny Plain and Twopence Coloured* (though prices have changed since his

day). With the highly ornamental theatre comes a choice of scenery and brightly-coloured cut-out figures for a number of plays, together with a book of the words they should speak.

Pollock's shop (which is also a toy museum) sells hundreds of other imaginative things, many revived from times past, and here are some they can supply by post:

'How to dress an old-fashioned doll' is a book with cutting-out diagrams, stitches, etc. for doll's clothes in the pretty styles of over seventy years ago.

Easy-to-make felt glove-puppets, which you cut out and stitch – choose from Punch, Judy and the policeman, a golliwog or a 'pearly queen'.

Pollock's own scrapbook is very decorative, and full of ideas like how to make skeleton leaves, glitter pictures, thumbprints, pressed ferns, spatter pictures, feather decorations, marbled paper, silhouettes, dried seaweed, ink-blot pictures and puzzle lettering.

Old-fashioned rag dolls to cut out and sew – these are called Lizzie and Jack. Also a handsome cat, William Henry.

A blank jigsaw, 25 × 30 cm, on which to paint a picture yourself. (Suggestion: paint birthday greetings, take it apart, and give it to a friend or parent as a birthday present.)

If you have a doll's house, you may like to wallpaper the rooms with special tiny-patterned papers.

A book of paper dolls to colour and cut out, including Queen Elizabeth I and her courtiers. Others in the series feature Henry VIII and his wives, Great Women, and Soldiers of the American Revolution (two books – British and American).

A Victorian parlour, with furniture and people to stand in it. This is another colour-and-cut book.

Buried treasure!

Buried or sunk, the lure of lost jewels and pieces of eight fascinates every treasure-seeker. Would you like a crackling parchment map that looks and feels really old, showing many of the places where the hoards of pirates and buccaneers are said to be still lost or hidden?

This is just one of many fascinating maps from Porter Prints. They specialise in producing exact copies of ancient maps and documents, printed on crisp, brownish paper that is just like old parchment. It's best to ask for their long list (send a stamped addressed envelope) before you make a choice. You might like an old map of your town or county the way it was 200, 300 or 400 years ago. Or perhaps you'd like Captain Cook's own map of the South Sea Islands. A very interesting one that has been made up shows every single attempt at invasion or civil war in England and Wales since William the Conqueror.

Then there are the historical documents and posters, which include things like the reward posters for famous outlaws – Ned Kelly of Australia, Jesse James of America, and others. You might like to start a collection.

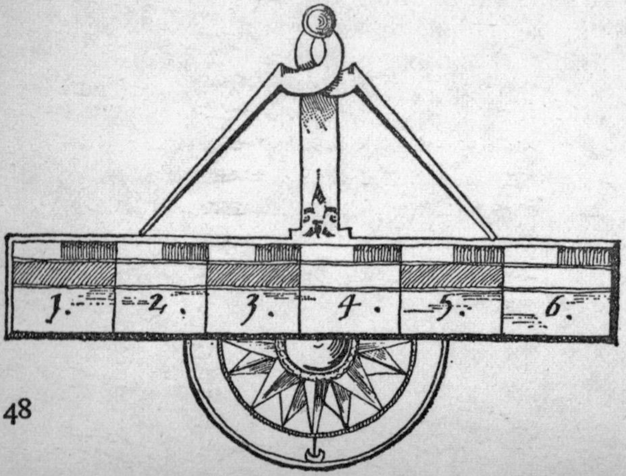

Sizzling sausages

A colourful leaflet tells all about sausages, from pig to pan! Did you know the ancient Greeks ate them, and that the modern Britons eat six thousand million a year? You can have the leaflet FREE (together with other leaflets, some containing recipes) if you send a stamped addressed envelope to: *British Sausage Bureau, 26 Fitzroy Square, London W1P 6BT.*

Here's an unusual recipe called Dublin Coddle. As you may guess it comes from Ireland, where it used to be cooked over a peat fire in cottages of days gone by. It's a splendidly warming hotpot.

Prick 500 g sausages here and there with a fork. Peel and slice 500 g onions. Peel and quarter 500 g potatoes. Put these ingredients into a deep saucepan with a thick base, add 500 ml milk and bring slowly to the boil. Simmer gently over a low heat for 1½ hours or until the potatoes are soft and breaking up. Stir carefully from time to time to prevent food sticking to the bottom of the pan. If a wide saucepan is used the milk will evaporate quicker and it may be necessary to add a little more. When the contents of the pan have turned into a lovely thick creamy stew, it is ready. The spicy sausage will flavour the gravy, but you may wish to add a little more salt.

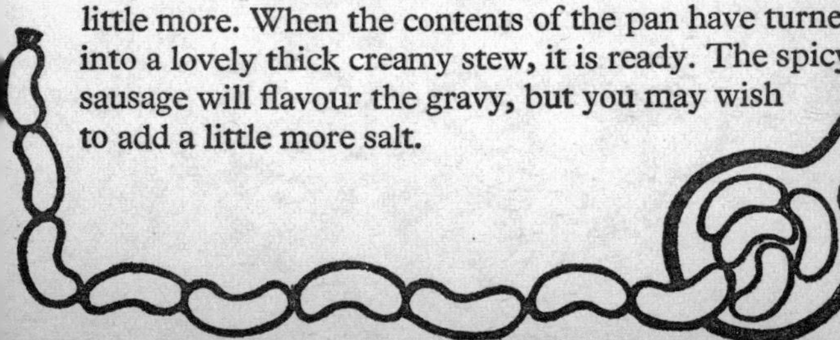

Planning a party?

In London there is a fantastic shop called Barnums, which sells every imaginable kind of decoration, mask, balloon, funny hat, carnival novelty, wig, flag, cracker or garland you might need to make a party go with a swing. Their huge catalogue is so fabulous that they don't give it away free but lend it to you instead. They ask you to send a deposit, but this is returned to you as soon as you post the catalogue back. One of the best buys is a carton of twenty-four assorted hats (two of each design): crowns, bonnets, pierrot's, hussar's, sailor's, highwayman's and others.

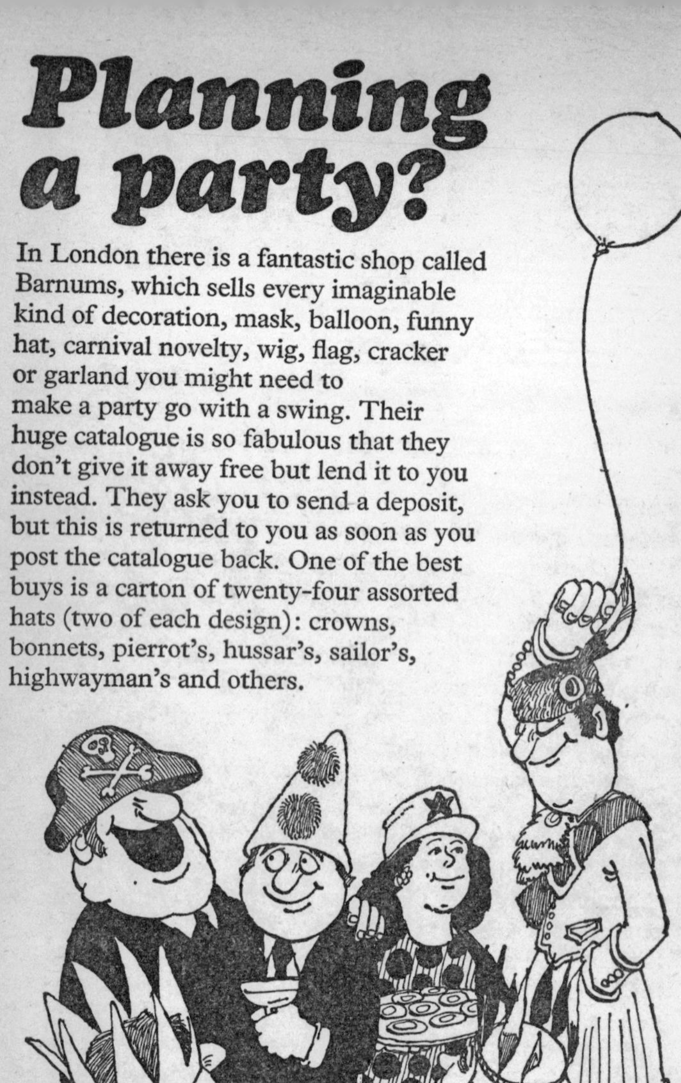

Pets galore

Do you keep a pet? If it's one of the following, you may like to know where you can get a leaflet about taking good care of it – how to feed and house it and how to keep it in good health.

rats and mice	hamsters	hedgehogs
aquarium fish	rabbits	budgerigars
dogs	tortoises	horses and ponies
terrapins	gerbils	cats

These leaflets are available FREE to anyone who joins the National Pets Club, run by the Daily Mirror. Over ½ million children and adults have joined and received a badge, free voucher tickets to a whole number of zoos up and down the country, and the opportunity to get any advice they may need about their pets.

Did you know hedgehogs make friendly pets? A hedgehog soon loses its shyness. They are easiest to catch at dusk, wearing thick gloves (don't pick up by the spines – that's cruel). A hedgehog needs a big wire cage with a covered top (hedgehogs can climb as well as burrow) and a wooden house for the night and to hibernate in during winter. If you don't want to hunt for worms and slugs to feed your hedgehog, buy tinned dog meat and give it root vegetables too. If you keep a boar and a sow (husband and wife hedgehogs), separate them while the sow is having her babies, for the jealous father may kill them. You may need an insecticide powder to get rid of the fleas most hedgehogs have.

Historical costume

Clothes of the past are as fascinating as they are beautiful or strange, and a number of museums now have fabulous displays of treasures, sometimes saved from the ragbag in the nick of time. (Anything overlooked in *your* gran's attic, do you suppose?)

You could spend many a happy hour colouring pictures of clothes to hang on your bedroom wall, for the Museum of Costume in Bath has produced some pictures intended for just that purpose.

The Museum sells a pad of fashion designs of the 1830s – reproductions of the originals, each one 15×21 cm. There are thirty of them, and they would look like genuine old fashion-plates if you water-coloured them in delicate tints.

The Museum also has two sheets of little figures, 'Fashion Outlines', 1880–1913 and 1914–1969, which shows you how fashions changed almost year by year. These, too, are for colouring.

Star gymnasts

It makes you feel exhausted just to look at it! A huge fold-out poster (double-sided), crowded with colour photos of the world's top gymnasts! This action-packed sheet not only shows all the most famous names in the Olympics and world gymnastics generally, with full details of their achievements, but has a reference section with statistics of all the medallists of 1976 at Montreal. It's sold

to raise money for the Jaffa Gym Fund, by the way, which was set up to provide better training facilities for young gymnasts. From the same source come big photo posters (about 60 × 90 cm) of four stars: Olga Korbut, Ludmila Tourischeva, Eberhard Geinger and Alex Detiatin, each in full colour and full action. You can also get a set of eight postcards of star gymnasts.

Men of the sea

This drawing is taken from a poster which shows a slice through a merchant ship with all the activity that goes on inside it, from the captain's bridge down to the boiler room. You can buy it for a very low price from The Marine Society, which is an organisation that helps seamen pass their free time on long voyages by studying. It also arranges for schools to 'adopt' different ships (merchant or Naval), correspond with them, and receive visits or possibly visit the ships themselves when they are in a home port. (Perhaps your geography teacher knows about this.)

From the same source you can get wallcharts such as one that explains all about container ships – how they work, what they carry, where they go, their crew and so on. Another deals with events on the voyage of a cargo ship to South America and back.

Country parks

That's the name for countryside kept specially for you near the town where you live. At least, that's the general idea – so far, about a hundred cities and towns have country parks near them, and more are being set up. They are open to the public, and if you want to know all about them and where they are you should write off for a paperback guide (with photos), available free from the Countryside Commission.

Because the parks vary so much, the guide tells you what each has to offer – a reservoir, a sea beach, fishing, golf, a barbecue site, nature trails, swimming, forest walks, ponds, canoeing, bird-watching, rock-climbing, tobogganing, camping – even a canal water-bus in one and an old cotton-mill in another!

The address to write to is:

The Countryside Commission, John Dower House, Crescent Place, Cheltenham, Glos GL50 3RA

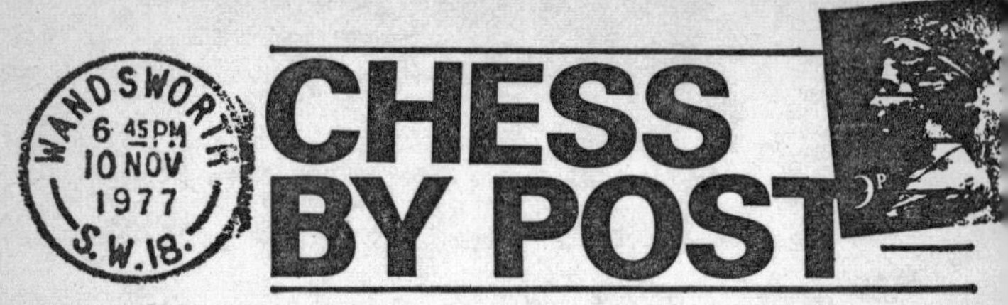

CHESS BY POST

If, like some children, you've a gift for playing chess, you may like the idea of being put in touch with someone who will play it with you by post. There's a club for such people, and it has made a very generous offer to readers of this book: if you want to join it they will reduce the annual subscription to £2 and also provide a free scorecard and window envelope package to start you off.

You write down each move as you make it on one of the scorecards and post it off to your opponent in a window envelope. He does likewise, and so it goes on. Admittedly a slow way to play chess, but it gives you lots of time to think out your moves and improve your game.

Membership of the club also entitles you to enter various types of tournament and, more important, you will be sent free gradings (How Good Are You?) every three months.

Interested? Then send your £2 subscription (or a stamp for further details) to:

The Peckham Postal Chess Club,
55 Blenheim Grove, London S.E.15

FREE!

London's Transport

Have you ever thought much about the bus or Underground train that takes you to school, for instance?

Your journey will be much more interesting if you read a very well produced 32-page paperback in red and black called 'What is London Transport?' It's about the history of how it all began in 1829 and the present and future too. Do you know how many kilometres London buses and tube trains travel in a year, how many passengers are carried, and how many bits of lost property are collected? Answers: 630 million; 1919 million; and over 156 thousand.

The longest tunnel is over 27 kilometres, the deepest station is 58.5 metres below ground level, the fastest lift whizzes up and down at 245 metres a minute, and the busiest (or should one say bussiest?) spot in London is Hyde Park Corner, which has 530 buses an hour passing through at peak periods. This fascinating book comes from:

Publicity Officer, London Transport, 280 Old Marylebone Road, London NW1 5RJ

'Save these Flowers'

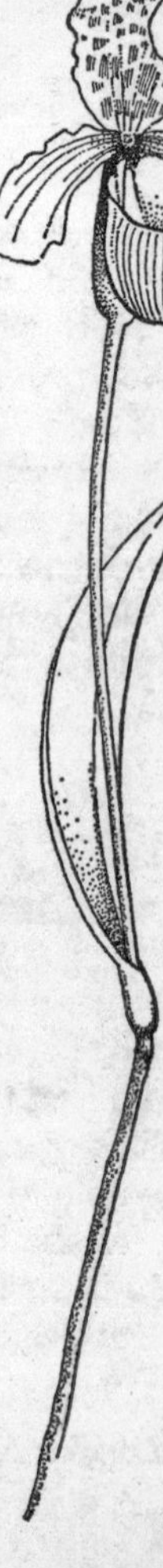

'These Endangered Plants are Protected by Law' is the name of a very pretty wallchart which illustrates twenty-one of the rarest wild flowers in Britain – ones you'll be very lucky to find in the countryside, and which on no account should be picked. Photograph them or draw them as a permanent record of your 'find'. Write and tell the Botanical Society about it, particularly if you think the rare flower is in any danger. Road-building, ploughing, the spread of fertilisers, planting forests of trees – all these can destroy the conditions needed for our wild flowers to survive.

Remember it is actually *illegal* to pick or uproot any of our twenty-one rarest plants and did you know it is also illegal to uproot *any* wild plant, unless it is on your own land?

The rare wild flowers protected by law are: Lady's Slipper (shown here), Monkey Orchid, Mezereon (also known as Daphne), Spiked Speedwell, Alpine Sow-Thistle, Red Helleborine, Cheddar Pink, Military Orchid, Wild Gladiolus, Alpine Gentian, Tufted and Drooping Saxifrage, Diapensia, Blue Heath, Snowdon Lily, Alpine Woodsia, Ghost Orchid, Killarney Fern, Oblong Woodsia, Spring Gentian and Teesdale Sandwort.

FREE!

Karoline the Kow

This particular cow spells herself with a K because she comes from Denmark. Very smart she is, in red and white with a tasty daisy in her mouth.

Karoline reaches you as a press-out cardboard model to assemble yourself. All you have to do to get her is write to the Danish Agricultural Producers. They will also send you free recipe leaflets using bacon, cheese, butter and other good things produced in Denmark.

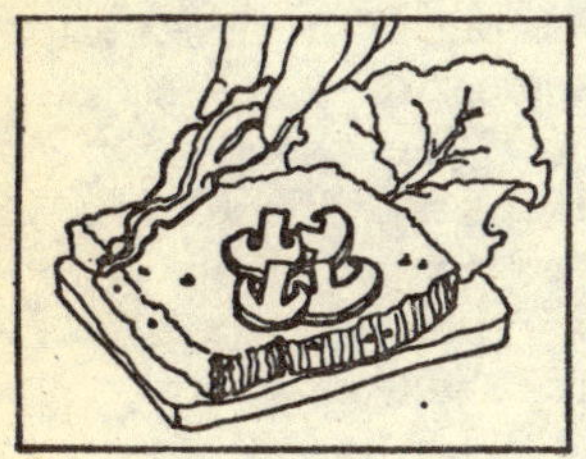

One of them tells you how to make 'Danwiches' – Danish-style sandwiches. These are open-topped, and the Danes themselves call them *smørrebrød*, which means buttered bread – for that's the basis of all of them. It's up to you what you put on top – any tasty mixture is right provided it's piled up, looks pretty and tastes good.

The address is write to is:

The Danish Agricultural Producers, Department C,
2–3 Conduit Street, London W1R 0AT

Along the Clipper Way

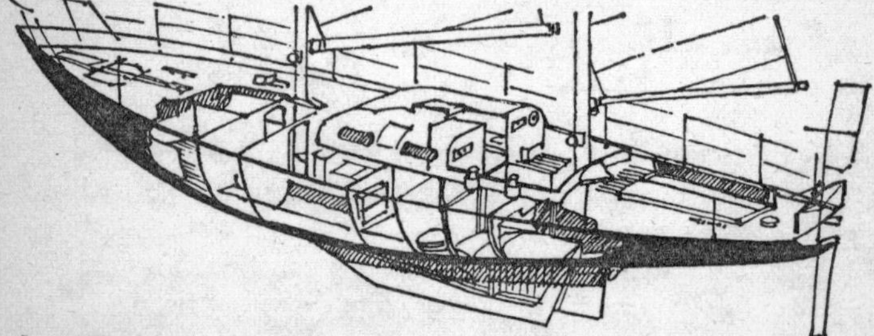

A really big, colourful wallchart tells the story of two famous ships – their design, history and the people who sailed them. One was the *Cutty Sark* and the other *Gipsy Moth IV*.

Cutty Sark, launched in 1869, was one of the famous huge sailing clippers which used to race at record speeds through the great oceans of the world. She was named after a dancing witch in the story of Tam O'Shanter. Every detail of this famous ship is on this wallchart together with dozens of drawings and photographs illustrating life on board, the hazards she used to encounter, the gear she carried, the men who sailed her, her route, figurehead, cargo – even the hens which supplied the captain with breakfast eggs get a place!

Also on the chart is *Gipsy Moth IV*, which in 1966 followed the same challenging route round the world via South Africa and Cape Horn. She was sailed single-handed by Francis Chichester, who was later knighted for this achievement – no man had done it this way before. He was a youngster of sixty-five at the time! The chart illustrates his ketch in great detail. Remember that you can visit both *Gipsy Moth IV* and *Cutty Sark* at Greenwich by the Thames in London.

FREE!

Other people's lives

A government department is giving away booklets, some of which open up to make posters, each describing a different tropical country. They are all countries to which Britain gives money and other aid, because their peoples do not enjoy as good a standard of living as we do. The photographs in the booklets show what progress is being made with (for example) introducing new crops to provide food, helping to find customers overseas for other crops, building airports or ships or radio stations, using new machinery, and so on.

Which of these developing countries interests you most?

African countries – The Gambia, Malawi, Botswana, Swaziland, Lesotho
Asian countries – India, Malaysia, Nepal
South America – Guyana
Islands – Solomon Islands, St Lucia, Fiji, Mauritius, Seychelles.

Write for booklets to:

Information Dept, The Ministry of Overseas Development, Eland House, Stag Place, London SW1E 5DH

Is it a money~box?

Or is it a purse? You can use it either way, because it's small enough to carry in your pocket and yet can hold a great many coins. This clever double-sided gadget is called a Flip-O-Coin.

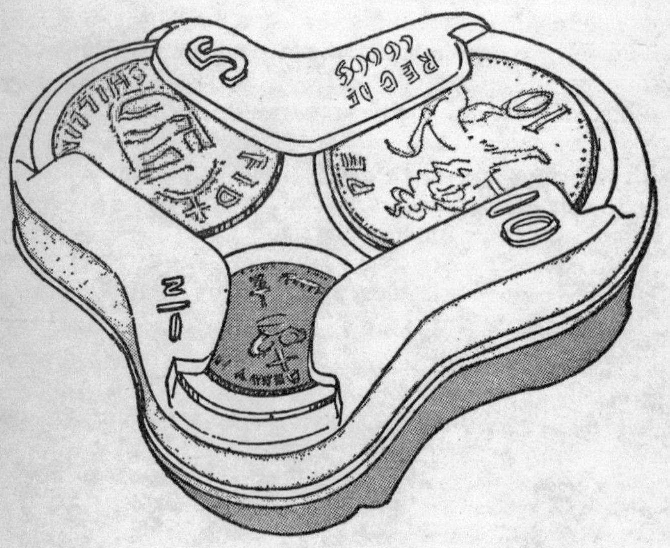

It has spaces to fit $\frac{1}{2}$p, 1p, 2p, 5p, 10p and 50p coins. You can press in as many (almost!) coins as you like, and just slide out one at a time as needed. You can see at a glance what coins you've got.

This clever invention is so ingenious that everyone stops to stare when you produce it to pay your bus fare or buy some sweets.

Posters unlimited

Would you like to be let into a secret? Where do all those super posters come from which your teachers pin up on classroom walls?

Some at least are given away FREE in a magazine which many teachers read, called 'Child Education'. This comes out every month and always contains a poster. Every two months 'Child Education Special' is published, complete with a really outsize one.

You too could obtain these posters by getting the magazines. The Special issue is particularly interesting because it always has stories, poems, projects and things to make connected with the subject of the poster – whether it is ships, flowers, dinosaurs, snow . . . or any other subject. It's always packed with good things, like this idea for a hanging plant-bottle. It came from an issue of the magazine which was about gardens and gardening and which, as usual, had a splendid poster that might have cost two or three times more if bought from a shop.

British uniforms

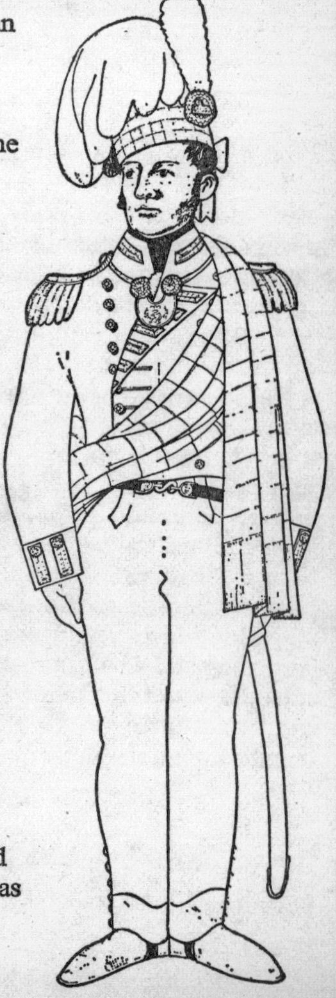

The National Army Museum can send you their colouring sheets with officers or men of many historic regiments. Each is 19×28 cm and has a clear outline for you to fill in with paint or felt-tip pen. To help you get things right exact details are given of the correct colours to use, even down to belts and boots. The splendid gentleman shown here is an officer from the 42nd (Royal Highland) Regiment of Foot, 1815.

Other regiments you can choose from are:

Grenadier Guards 1829
83rd Foot, 1855
West Leicester Militia, 1814
Royal Horse Artillery, 1815
2nd (Royal North British) Dragoons, 1815
10th (Prince of Wales' Own Royal) Hussars, 1815

If you're a real enthusiast for military things, ask for a FREE copy of the Museum's sales list, which has fifteen pages crammed with things you can order, such as pictures, books, model soldiers, postcards, slides and jigsaws.

Neptune in colour

In the Corinium Museum at Cirencester is a very ancient Roman mosaic floor excavated in modern times. It shows the head of Neptune, god of the sea and rivers (not far from Cirencester is the source of the River Thames).

That mosaic has now been adapted to make a rather unusual colouring project which you can do. Each little square has been printed and its correct colour indicated. Fastened on top of the whole picture is some thick tracing paper. When you've done your colouring on the tracing paper, you can hang Neptune up where the light will shine through and make your colours glow.

The same Museum sells other nice things, like replicas of Roman coins made into finger-rings to wear, and sets of five Roman coins or eight mediaeval ones. The sets are mounted in boxes. They can send you a list of all the goods they sell by post.

World families

This is the title of a set of particularly attractive wall charts, coloured all over, each about 60 cm wide and 40 cm high. There are eight in all, and they would make a lovely frieze pinned round your walls.

Each tells the story of how one particular family lives, such as Ali, a farmer in Morocco. He goes to market to sell his vegetables and pay taxes. He and his family wear loose, cool clothes to protect them from the heat, and Mrs Ali wears a veil. Ploughing is done by hand, and much of the wheat grown has to be given to their landlord. Ali prays in the mosque then drinks mint tea sitting on the floor of a friend's house. When he gets home, riding on his donkey, there will be a stew of semolina, peas and olives for dinner.

Other countries featured in these picture stories are India, Bolivia, Jamaica, China, Nigeria, Brazil and Indonesia.

Your camera

You'll get better results if you take a few tips on photography from the experts. And who is likely to know more than Kodak, the camera people?

They have dozens of information leaflets on every kind of camera problem right up to professional level, and you can have up to six of them if you send the postage cost (20p postal order or stamps). You can get a list, but a good selection for a young photographer might be:

picture-taking in five minutes, for all the basic know-how;
tips for better pictures;
better pictures next time;
photographing sporting events;
better camping pictures.

Would you like to know how photography began, and see some of the rare exhibits Kodak have in their museum and among their old records? Or learn a bit about the scientific side, clearly explained in brightly coloured diagrams? All this, plus some information about the uses of photography in map-making, space research, dentistry and many other fields is in a very readable booklet called 'Photography'. It also tells how to process your own prints. Kodak's address is:

Kodak Ltd, Customer Relations, P.O. Box 66, Station Road, Hemel Hempstead HP1 1JU

OLD TRANSPORT

Several museums have special collections of old forms of transport, including the Merseyside one. This Museum has produced some interesting items for enthusiasts, such as colour-and-cut cardboard models to assemble yourself. One of these is the old 'Lion' locomotive built in 1838, in the early days of steam (it was the tall-chimneyed loco that you saw in the film 'The Titfield Thunderbolt'). Another is the steel paddle-steamer *Hope*, built in 1864 and used as a Confederate blockade runner during the American Civil War. Alas, her steam-pipe burst on a return journey, and she was captured.

The Museum also has old maps of Liverpool, including a bird's eye view drawn from a balloon in 1885, and many interesting prints in lovely delicate colours. Two of these are 'The Landing Stage, 1880', with three paddle-steamers and a schooner in the foreground, and a quaint early railway scene showing two engines and fifteen carriages trundling along crammed with top-hatted or bonneted passengers. Both these prints are an interesting shape, long and panoramic.

Don't forget!

1 Write your name and address clearly and say exactly what you want

2 Send the correct money in stamps or postal orders (not cash)

3 Enclose a big enough stamped addressed envelope, if required

4 Address your envelope correctly and stamp it

Get glueing!

Here's a little book with a lot of ideas for things that are easy to make at home, and fun too (even though it's called 'Classroom Crafts'). Among its contents are papier mâché models and glove puppets, book-covers, paper mosaics, jigsaw maps, 3-D pictures, a model village, Easter and Christmas ideas, cardboard astronauts, a fish mobile, finger puppets, collage, picture frames made from cartons, decorated boxes, and this idea for making a paper mask:

You cut holes for the eyes and mouth in a paper bag large enough to go over your head, and glue paper eyelashes on to it. Ears and nose are also cut from paper and glued on. Finally, lots of paper-strip curls can be added for hair. Use paint or big felt-tip pens for colouring the features.

By Golly!

Robertsons, the jam people, also sell other things which you may care to have if you like the Golly character who appears on their jars, because they are very good value. To order any of these items, you also have to collect two paper Gollies from the jars.

There are brilliantly coloured PVC aprons and bags (for your swimming things, school books, etc.), bright red and green with Golly to the fore; Golly himself (a 45-cm doll); fabric hats – blue and white baseball or white beanie styles; red, white and blue stretch belts for jeans and Golly T-shirts. There's a FREE leaflet showing all these things and more, which you can look at before ordering.

Introducing Effie

Effie the Effluent is the heroine of a strip-cartoon book about water and the problems of pollution. Write to your local water authority. If they don't have this book they will send you other free leaflets, and you can get your copy of Effie from the National Water Council at

1 Queen Anne's Gate, London SW1H 9BT

Sheep-spotter's guide

You may think you know a sheep when you see one, but do you know *which* sheep it is ? Can you tell a Suffolk from a Blackface or a Romney from a Dorset Horn ? There are over thirty breeds of sheep in Britain.

You can get a big full-colour poster from the British Wool Marketing Board, showing forty breeds of British sheep, which would make a colourful splash on your bedroom wall. The forty breeds are also illustrated in a book called 'British Sheep Breeds', which tells you where each one is raised and what its wool is used for. This book is aimed at older readers, but for the younger age-range there is 'Three Bags Full', which describes, with pictures, the visit of two children to a farm on sheep-shearing day. After watching the shearing they go with the farmer to the wool-merchant's, where the wool is weighed and sorted, and then visit the mill, where it is washed and dyed and put through the carding machine, which combs out all the tangles, before being spun and woven.

If you would like the sheep poster or either of the books, write to the British Wool Marketing Board. Its address and all the prices are given in the back of the book.

Are you a dog-lover?

If you like dogs, get yourself a copy of the official picture-chart of the Dog Spotters Club, which has colour drawings of nearly a hundred different breeds. See how many you know, and tick off each unfamiliar one as you spot it.

When you buy this chart you will be helping the National Canine Defence League, which exists to look after lost or unwanted dogs. They sell other things too, like doggy tea towels, greetings cards, books on the care of dogs and gear for dogs – from collars to cushions. Ask for a list. They will also send you FREE their newspaper, published twice a year.

Fred Basset's on the scent

'The hound that's almost human', they call him. Maybe you already follow Fred's antics in the *Daily Mail* and on TV, but did you know you can buy the strip cartoons in books now? The latest is *Fred Basset* No. 29.

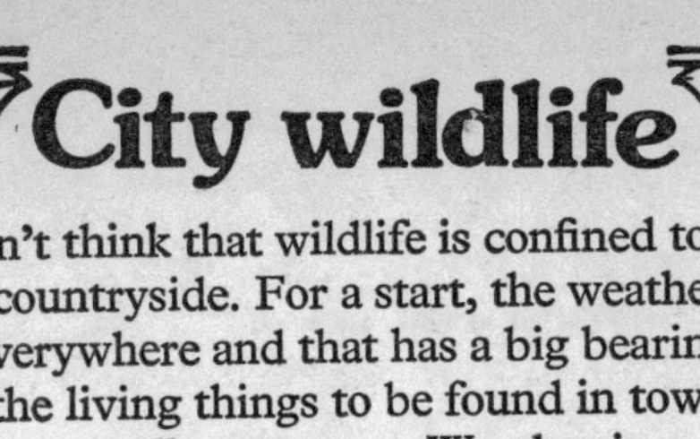

City wildlife

Don't think that wildlife is confined to the countryside. For a start, the weather is everywhere and that has a big bearing on the living things to be found in town as well as country. Weather is a fascinating subject in itself. And wherever you live there is life teeming around you – under paving stones or in the cracks of walls, on rubbish tips or waste areas, in window-boxes and water butts, beside paths and in park trees, in ponds and in gutters, among the grasses in the lawn. Bird-watching, making a wormery, recording wild flowers and the winged insects they attract, doing bark-rubbings or taking plaster-casts, analysing soil, setting up a bird-table, collecting crawling insects in a pooter – these are some of the things you can do if you want to be an amateur naturalist in town. There is an excellent thirty-page book to give you lots of ideas and know-how, which you can send for, called 'Nature in Your Town'. From the same source comes a record, 'Birds in Your Garden', which combines a talk with sound effects to help you recognise two familiar birds' songs – those of the chaffinch and the great tit. It was made by the famous bird mimic, Percy Edwards, whom you may have heard on radio or TV.

pottery at home

Maybe you enjoy working with clay in craft lessons at school. It's a hobby you can practise at home too, and if you use one of the new self-hardening clays, you don't need a kiln.

You can order ColdClay (and ColdGlazes too) from a pottery. It's real clay, not an imitation, and comes ready for modelling. When it's hard it can be painted, or if you leave it unpainted it's possible later to soften it for re-use on some other project. If you put glaze on, this will give a shiny and water-resistant finish.

The Pottery also has a FREE pamphlet about making clay pots, models and other things using ColdClay and ColdGlaze, with some ideas on how to decorate pottery too.

If you get really keen, you might like a set of their pottery work cards, which are large and beautifully produced, with a shiny wipe-clean surface, setting out very clearly how to do all kinds of interesting things with clay.

‘There she blows!’

That was the traditional cry of the old-time whalermen when they sighted one of these great sea-creatures spouting, and they would chase after with their harpoons at the ready. Men and beasts were fairly equally matched in the contest then, but modern whalers with their electrically operated harpoon guns have slaughtered so many whales that fewer and fewer are left each year. Will there soon be none?

‘Whales: the Threatened Giants of our Seas’ is a big wall poster showing nine of the thirty species that are known, from the smallest (the 9-metre Minke) to the largest, which is in fact the biggest animal that has ever inhabited the earth (the 30-metre Blue Whale).

These creatures are hunted not only for their fat but for other parts too: even their tendons are used for some tennis-racket strings. The chart, which appeared when the World Wildlife Fund started its 1977–78 campaign to conserve sea creatures, asks everyone to read labels and avoid buying products made from whales, if they can.

FREE!

Paper capers

You'll be surprised how many things you can make out of (guess what!) toilet paper, kitchen paper and paper handkerchiefs. Their cardboard rolls and boxes come in useful too.

Bowater-Scott (who make Andrex, Scotties and other paper things) have a set of twelve leaflets which give step-by-step instructions for making the following things: a Christmas tree and fairy, crackers, a bauble, a Christmas angel, parcel wrappings, table decorations, bangles, napkin rings, decorations, a hanging bird, paper flowers of many kinds, animals, an Easter chick, a mobile, funny men and an octopus.

If you want these 'Paper Capers', write to:

Bowater-Scott (Consumer Information Service),
East Grinstead House, East Grinstead, Sussex

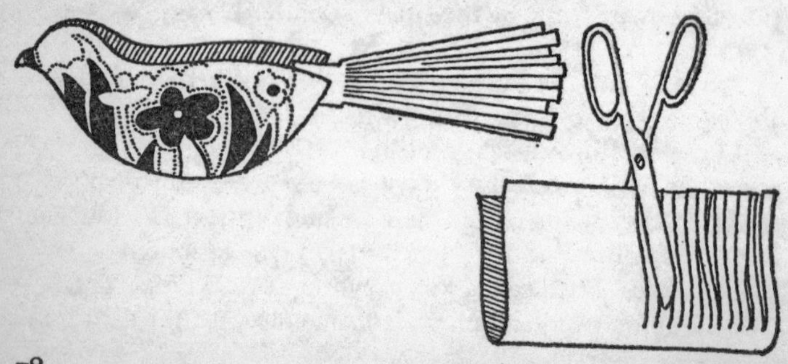

Pick of the posters

London Transport has always produced really first-rate posters, and so many people started asking whether they could obtain copies to hang up like pictures that London Transport decided to put the best of them on sale. You can examine them in a fascinating catalogue in which each poster is shown the size of a postage stamp. Unfolded, the catalogue itself makes a very good wallchart.

When asked to pick out the ones most popular with children, they chose:

'Children's London' – a riot of red and gold merry-go-round horses;

'The Londoners' Transport through the Ages' – a long cavalcade from Roman chariots and litters down to the 'tube' of today;

a comical poster first issued in 1908: 'No Need to Ask a P'liceman'.

The catalogue mentioned above includes these posters and dozens more, plus other things for bus and train enthusiasts – transport postcards, books, pictures on blockboard, and details of 100,000 (yes!) photographs, model buses, badges, wall plaques and jigsaws.

Industry at work

Some big companies are glad to send you well-produced booklets or wallcharts explaining how things are made. If you're interested in technical matters, and perhaps might make a career in industry one day, it's always worth writing to enquire. Here are a couple of examples of products vitally important to our modern world for its fuel and for its buildings: oil and cement.

If you're keen on seeing the way oil is piped from the bed of the sea, and if you're good at assembling cardboard models, there's a set of three to be had, called 'Sea Quest', which includes an exploration oil rig, a support ship and a pipe-laying barge.

'Blue Circle Cement' is much more interesting than you might suppose. A free sixteen-page book with particularly clear, brightly-coloured drawings tells you all about cement in pictures – how the chalk is quarried, the processes of manufacture, how cement gives strength to concrete, the sort of buildings that are made with it, what is done to prevent it polluting the air, and much else.

Time to wash

Maybe washing your face isn't your favourite occupation, but here's something that adds a lot of fun to it – a beautifully drawn and gaily coloured frieze to put up in your bedroom. It's over 150 cm long and 25 cm high, and shows the activities of a whole family of children throughout the day. To get it, all you need to do is to send a 10p stamp to:

Council of British Ceramic Sanitaryware Manufacturers, Federation House, Stoke-on-Trent ST4 2RT

Don't forget!

1 Write your name and address clearly and say exactly what you want

2 Send the correct money in stamps or postal orders (not cash)

3 Enclose a big enough stamped addressed envelope, if required

4 Address your envelope correctly and stamp it

Young Rescue

There are quite a number of clubs you can join by post (read my paperback *Joining Things*, published by Pan), but one in particular is both unusual and interesting. It's for young people of 9–16 who care about archaeology and our distant past. A really well written newsletter keeps you informed about all sorts of new discoveries, the badge and membership card gain you admission to some sites where 'digs' are in progress, and there are holidays, projects, competitions and a Young Rescue T-shirt. You may be able to join in flint-chipping or bread-baking by Iron Age methods. The subscription is £1.50 a year. Send it to:

Young Rescue, New Hall, Cambridge CB3 0DF

How it used to be

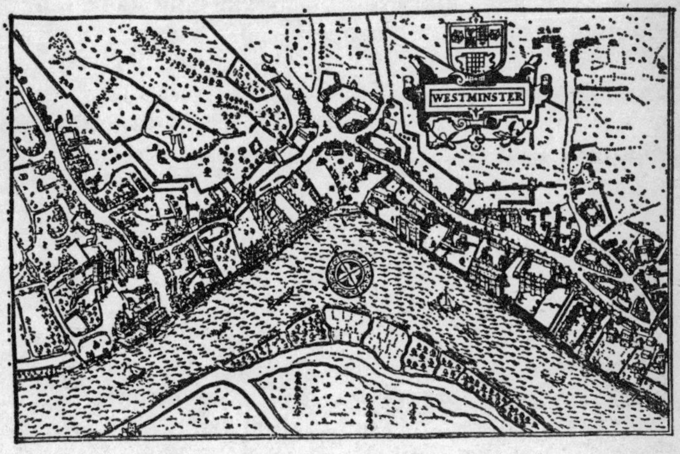

Most maps showed very little detail of places until in 1803 the first one-inch-to-a-mile maps from the Ordnance Survey started to appear. It took nearly seventy years for the whole country to be mapped.

It may be fascinating, if you enjoy maps, to obtain one of these old ones for your area and compare present times with what is shown on the map of 100–170 years ago. The old ones have recently been reprinted. You may find railway lines have appeared or vanished, that where there are now busy streets, there was once a farm, or that what is now a tiny park was once part of a nobleman's large estate.

For ship enthusiasts

If you're really keen on ships and have read every book you can lay hands on, filled your room with ship models, and covered the walls with pictures of ships – what next? The answer is ship profiles.

Each profile is a kind of kit – a fat wallet packed with first-hand details about one particular ship and all sorts of inside information you won't get anywhere else.

Take, for instance, the profile of *Southampton Castle*, the most powerful cargo liner in the world. Open up her wallet and the first thing you will find is a big cutaway diagram of the ship to hang on the wall, giving a glimpse of everything that goes on above and below decks, from the workings of the radar-scanner down to the rudder. There's a sheet of silhouettes and data of all her sister ships in the 'Castle' fleet; lots of photos; the history of mail ships, and another of the Clan line; charts and information about her home port, Southampton; the diary of a fortnight's voyage to South Africa; her crew list, and what they all do; even the officers' menus for a day! The cargoes carried to and fro are described, and there's a packet of information on career opportunities. Along with this comes a stack of colourful brochures about the countries *Southampton Castle* visits, and their products which she carries home to Britain – fruit, gold, wine and much else.

Two other ships have had their profiles compiled in a similar way – *Diomed* (trading in the Far East) and *British Inventor* (an oil tanker, voyaging between Japan and Britain), combined with a profile of the smaller tanker *British Poplar* (following a route in the Baltic).

A tiger, an elephant and a rabbit

Three good friends for younger children! They're to be found on a set of pretty posters (green, orange and blue) to pin on a bedroom or bathroom wall, each with a message about how to take good care of one's teeth. The same friendly characters turn up in a kit called 'The Party' – inside is a story booklet, a long wall-frieze to colour, sticky pictures to press out and fix in place, a lot of colouring sheets together with crayons, and some card models to make up. A good many hours' play in all that!

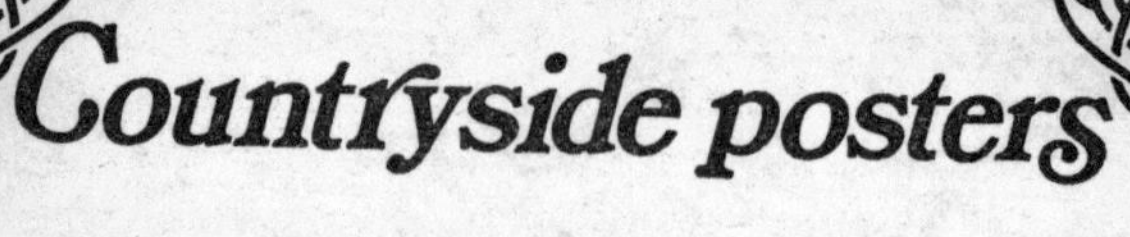

Countryside posters

If you care about the fact that some of our loveliest places are being ruined by carelessness – litter, pollution and so forth – you may like to help the Council for the Protection of Rural England by buying some of its excellent posters, which would be a very decorative way to brighten up your room (or maybe you'd like to spread the message by hanging one or two at your windows). They come in sets, costing little more than buying some posters singly at shop prices.

If you like a 'pop' style, ask for their four pop posters of a clown, dandelion 'clocks', crushed daffodil and an art nouveau theme.

If you prefer something more informative, order the five 'concern for the countryside' charts, which feature colour drawings of wild life in each different habitat (woodland, urban, hedgerow, motorway and freshwater). Also shown with a warning red triangle are the kinds of litter that can maim or kill – pick up a bottle or plastic bag and you may save a life.

Sweet treats

If you like sweet things and you like cooking too, then the British Sugar Bureau has several things to offer you. (But since sweet things aren't good for your teeth, write off also for the tooth-care things mentioned in this book.)

There is a set of 12 big (20 × 25 cm), shiny, colourful and very clear cookery cards. On one side is a picture from a favourite story together with something to cook that goes with it (like Tuckshop Oatcakes for *Tom Brown's Schooldays* and Desert Island Bananas for *Treasure Island*). On the other side is a step-by-step picture strip showing you just how to prepare the dish. The set comes in a cardboard folder that turns into a stand on which you can prop up your card while you work.

The Bureau also has two lively sixteen-page books about the story of sugar – FREE. 'Crystals from the Sun' is for under-elevens and 'Energy from the Sun' for over-elevens. They're both very well illustrated, in colour. Did you know the word 'sugar' is Arabic? It was not till our Crusaders went to fight the Saracens that we learnt about the sugar the Arabs were already using. That's just some of the information in these books, which take the sugar story right up to our own space age.

Famous faces

If you want a portrait of your favourite person from the past – hero, writer, actor, monarch or explorer – the chances are that London's National Portrait Gallery will be able to help you, whether you'd like a small postcard or a full-scale poster. They have paintings of just about everybody who played a part in British history.

The Gallery also produces an unusual colouring book called 'People from the Past', featuring some celebrities from the 16th, 17th and 18th centuries. In each case, one page shows a photograph of a portrait that can be seen at the Gallery, together with a short account of the person's life, while on the opposite page is a rough outline based on the portrait which you can colour as you like – a fine book for anyone who enjoys history, or beautiful costumes, or art. When you've filled the book with colour, why not go and compare your efforts with the paintings in the National Portrait Gallery?

Don't forget!

1 Write your name and address clearly and say exactly what you want

2 Send the correct money in stamps or postal orders (not cash)

3 Enclose a big enough stamped addressed envelope, if required

4 Address your envelope correctly and stamp it

Down on the farm

You may often wonder what exactly goes on behind the scenes at a farm, especially if you live in a town. Why not go and see? The Association of Agriculture has made arrangements for certain farms to open their gates to the public on various dates of the year. To find out the nearest one to your home, all you need to do is write to the Association for its list of Farm Open Days, issued three times a year between April and October. They tell you not only how to get there, but what sort of things you will see. At one farm sheep-shearing may be in progress, at another milking, at a third horse-shoeing or bee-keeping demonstrations. Some charge a small sum to visitors, but many are free. You can't take your dog with you, and you should wear wellies. There may be tractor rides or the chance to eat or buy farm produce. Send one stamped addressed envelope per issue required to:

Farm Open Days, The Association of Agriculture,
16 Strutton Ground, London SW1P 2HP

Another list of farm trails, covering sixteen trails on working farms, comes from:

The Countryside Commission, John Dower House,
Crescent Place, Cheltenham, Glos. GL50 3RA

The greatest story in the world

If you think the Bible is merely something read *to* you, in church or school, think again! You're missing out on something. Apart from anything else, it contains some of the most action-packed stories in history or legend.

Here are two different ways of discovering the Bible for yourself.

One of the best strip cartoon books yet produced is called *Jesus and His Message of Liberation*. It's in full colour, and on glossy paper – 116 pages of drama. It was originally published in Paris but is now available in an English edition.

Another way to read the best bits of the Bible is to subscribe to 'Compass' – you'll get three copies in the course of a year. In each one, under the day's date, is a note telling you which short piece of the Bible you're recommended to read that day (in bed just before you go to sleep may be a good moment). 'Compass' then has a little bit to tell you about what you've just read. Sometimes the history of those times may be explained. Often the comments relate what you've just read to your own life here-and-now. Occasionally quizzes or puzzles are dropped in, or there are pictures to colour.

More pet-care leaflets

You only have to ask the People's Dispensary for Sick Animals and they will send you a leaflet about how to take good care of your pet, if it is one of the following:

canary	aquarium fish
dog	horse or pony
cat	parrot
tortoise	gerbil
budgerigar	hamster or mouse
rabbit or cavy (guinea-pig)	

Though these leaflets are free, the PDSA welcomes donations for its work or even gifts of trading stamps or used postage stamps, which it can sell.

Better still, you could join the PDSA's Animal Service Guild (for 11-to-18-year-olds) or Busy Bees (for under 11s). If you do this you will not only be able to help raise money for the PDSA's charitable work for animals in need, but you will receive a badge and a news magazine (very lively and readable) plus photo-posters, each with a big close-up of a favourite animal on it. All this is yours for a tiny subscription. The PDSA provides free veterinary treatment for sick and injured animals owned by people unable to afford private fees.

MAKING TOYS

Do you know about Toy Libraries? They've been set up all over the country for the use of childminders and foster parents and also to provide toys suitable for handicapped children to play with: there are over 600 libraries so far. In addition, they've got some small books about making toys, of interest to all children, whether handicapped or not, or to the parents of young ones not yet able to make things unaided. One is called 'Do It Yourself' and another is about 'Magnetic Board Toys'. The picture below shows one of the easy-to-make games from the first book – all you need is a long cardboard box to cut up and mark as shown, and a pingpong ball. The idea is to blow the ball as far up the slope as you can.

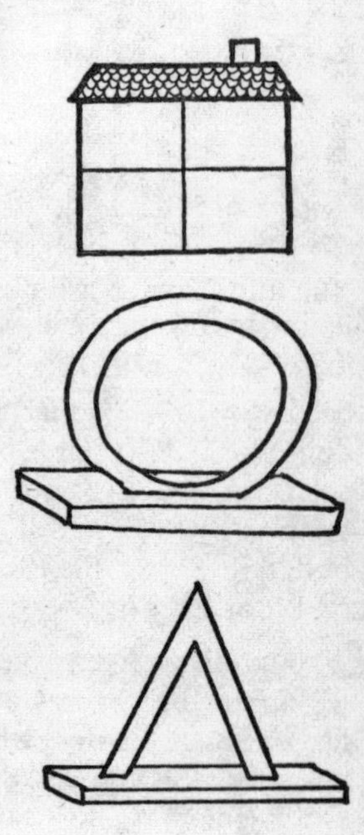

Hands Off These Animals!

This poster has colour photographs and information about six of Britain's rarest creatures – the sand lizard, smooth snake, natterjack toad, large blue butterfly, a very big horse-shoe bat, and the mouse-eared bat (with a dramatic picture of it in flight – there are, however, only a few dozen left in Britain). It is now illegal to interfere with any of these rare animals.

This poster comes from the Council for Nature, which will also send you a FREE specimen copy of their newsletter 'Habitat' to which you might like to subscribe, and a list of their other posters and publications. Enclose a stamped addressed envelope when writing for the newsletter or list or with any general enquiries.

7 GAMES AT A GO

Maybe your mother would get you this out of the housekeeping money, because it does double-duty as a very practical tablecloth (cotton coated with plastic that wipes clean).

On this brightly coloured cloth are laid out all the 'boards' you need to play snakes and ladders, tiddly-winks, ludo, draughts, chess, backgammon and a new racing game. It measures about 115 cm × 90 cm. The design is so lively that you may like to put the cloth up as a wall-hanging when not using it for playing games on the floor or serving tea on the table.

This bright idea comes from Clothkits, who also sell very good children's clothes cut out ready to sew together: they have a free catalogue of these.

Don't forget!

1 Write your name and address clearly and say exactly what you want

2 Send the correct money in stamps or postal orders (not cash)

3 Enclose a big enough stamped addressed envelope, if required

4 Address your envelope correctly and stamp it

45,000,000 years ago

Life in the Oligocene Period (that's long, long before man was known) is shown in a colourful chart of how the Isle of Wight probably looked then, complete with reptiles and some of the world's first mammals long since vanished. Fossilised remains of these creatures have been dug up, and you can even send for portions of them – bits of giant turtle shell, or of crocodile – and hold in your hand a little bit of life from 45,000,000 years ago!

TIN WHISTLE

Hornpipes, hymns, jigs or polkas – what's your fancy?

You've never blown a single note before? Then what you need is a Tin Whistle Kit. It contains a book of lessons, with fifteen tunes (easy ones first, of course), an eighteen-minute record or cassette keyed to the lessons, which demonstrates just how you should play, and, of course, the whistle itself.

The instructions are by two professional musicians who are expert tin-whistlers. The makers say firmly that the whole idea is fun not hard slog; you learn by playing, not by practising boring scales.

SOMETHING FISHY

Not just the fish we eat but the ships that catch them are featured on a small recipe leaflet called 'Some cheaper fish and how to cook them' – particularly interesting if you live near the sea.

The Choice is Ours

That's the title of four really fabulous big posters about protecting the wildlife of our country. Not only were top photographers used to take the really stunning close-ups, but the posters themselves are on glossy card that makes the colours glow.

There's one on butterflies and other winged insects, another on wild flowers, a third features birds, several of them at their nests, and the fourth some mammal fauna.

Of all the posters mentioned in this book, these are certainly the most spectacular, though they are moderately priced.

Make your own candles

This is a very pleasant hobby to have, and you can make candles for your own room (parents permitting – you don't want to set the house on fire), for the dinner table, for Christmas presents or to sell at school bazaars.

You can get a kit with enough materials in it to make seventeen candles – big, colourful, decorative ones. It contains wax and stearin, dyes in eight colours, wicks, two moulds and a step-by-step instruction book. If you haven't got a cookery thermometer at home, this too can be supplied.

Candle Makers Supplies, the firm which produces this kit, also sells separately all the equipment you need for making candles, so if you enjoy your first try at this fascinating hobby, there is plenty of scope for further experiment! You can buy moulds for all types of candle, including the chunky, embossed kind, but perhaps the most interesting are fruit-shaped moulds, from which you can make an apple, pear, orange, lemon, pepper, tomato, pineapple or bunch of grapes. The finished candles look amazingly like the real thing, and are perfumed to make them even more authentic!

For prices and details of the complete range available from Candle Makers Supplies, write to the address at the back of the book.

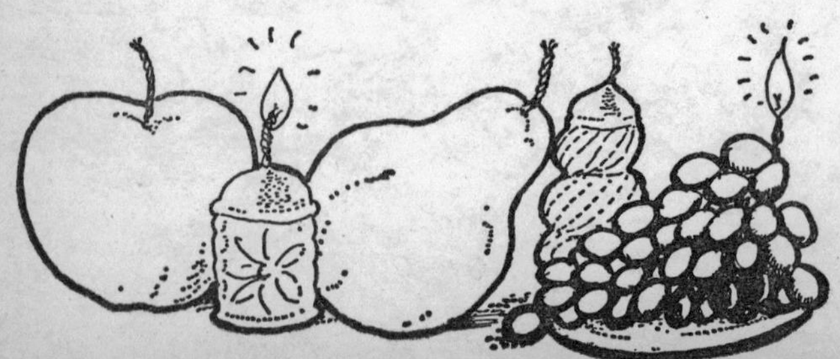

Art for the bone-idle

Nothing could be more 'instant' than rubber-stamping pictures: even big battle-scenes, for instance. All you do is gently press a picture-block on to an ink-pad and then on to paper. Babyish stuff? Not quite, because if you have a series of blocks with, say, soldiers in action in a variety of positions, you can create a really large and complicated landscape packed with action. Draw in some scenery and other effects yourself, then colour the whole lot. (What about a big mural on your bedroom wall, or a long frieze made on the back of a leftover roll of wallpaper?)

The choice of series available includes: aircraft, flowers, Xmas pictures, battle (World War 2), zoo animals, dinosaurs, farm and horses show-jumping.
You can use them not only to create pictures for colouring but also to make greetings cards, to stamp outlines on to fabric for embroidering, or to decorate things like paper plates and plain lampshades.

S.S. 'Great Britain'

Launched in 1843, the *Great Britain* was the first ocean-going ship made of iron and propeller-driven (not a paddle steamer). This historic vessel was rotting far away in a South Atlantic harbour until she was rescued in 1970 and the long task of restoring her began. She now has a permanent home in Bristol, where she was built, and it is possible to visit her.

When the famous engineer Brunel built her she was of a size never before known – 322 feet long (about 98 metres) – which was big enough to swallow two steamships then considered 'immense'. Prince Albert himself named and launched her, after six hundred people had banqueted on board, as the city's church bells rang out and flags fluttered everywhere. Guns were fired, stirring music played, and the golden arms of Britain shone on her black bow. She was so wide that she nearly stuck in a lock on the way out, and part of its walls had to be removed.

A worse disaster occurred three years later when, with

180 passengers on board, the *Great Britain* struck rocks near the Irish coast. Being made of iron, she survived a hazard that would have torn a wooden ship apart, although getting her off the rocks safely proved a long and difficult task. Her last voyage was in 1886, with a cargo of coal that caught fire near the Falkland Islands. She was condemned to lie rotting away for the best part of a century before being salvaged.

Even if you cannot visit her in Bristol, you can write to her souvenir shop for a list of *Great Britain* mementoes that you can buy by post. For instance, there's a fine ballpoint pen with a transparent top which shows the ship seemingly floating on the sea inside, a cardboard model to cut out and make up into an authentic replica of the ship, a poster and a T-shirt with the ship on it.

A really super, big picture of the *Great Britain* on her first voyage, taken from a painting of the time, is sold by the National Maritime Museum, who also have one of her launching.

Outings in London

If you want to know what to do in London, ask the London Tourist Board to send you information. Tell them what sort of things you are interested in and they will send you leaflets.

The London Tourist Board, 26 Grosvenor Gardens, London SW1

A Bus and Underground map, complete with a lot of information about sightseeing, is obtainable FREE at many tube stations, or you should write to:

London Transport, Broadway, London SW1

Your favourite foods

If you enjoy finding out about the good things we eat, such as where they come from and how they are cultivated, you may like to know where to get free booklets, wallcharts or posters about them. Here's a selection of some of the best and most colourful ones (you may find some helpful for school projects too).

Oranges 'The Story of Outspan' is a 24-page booklet full of vivid colour photographs telling the story of fruit-growing in South Africa (oranges, lemons and grapefruit). None of these fruits grew there until the Dutch settlers brought in some plants (from St Helena, the South Atlantic island where Napoleon was later to be exiled). Now there are vast orange groves in Africa. 'Outspan' comes from a Dutch word used to describe the unyoking of oxen at the end of a long day's trek – a time for refreshment. For a copy of the booklet write to:

Outspan House, High Street, Berkhamsted, Herts HP4 1AN

You may like to know that you can buy four special grapefruit spoons from Outspan. They have slender serrated tips that make it unnecessary to prepare grapefruit before serving, and cost only 55p a set – a present for Mum?

Butter and cheese A colourful leaflet ('Anchor in your week') gives a week's recipes using butter and cheese. Banana meat loaf, butter nut shortbread and rhubarb ginger crumble are just three of the delicious recipes for you to try. With this leaflet comes a booklet about dairy farming in New Zealand. This started in 1841, when a missionary brought two cows and a bull with him. Now over two million cows make the country's dairying one of its biggest industries. From:

Anchor Foods Limited, Bath Road, Swindon, Wilts.

Another country that's proud of its cheeses is Germany. You can get a big, colourful map to hang on your wall, which shows where each kind comes from, and they're all illustrated and described on the back. Write to:

The German Food Centre, 44 Knightsbridge, London SW1

Tea A shiny and cheerful wallchart in green and blue shows all the different parts of the world where tea is grown and how many million kilos come from each place, with photographs showing tea plantations, and how the leaves are picked, dried, crushed, baked, sifted and then transported to us. A little red book is also included, which answers just about every question you might have concerning tea, particularly its fascinating history. The Chinese were already enjoying tea-drinking more than a thousand years ago, but it did not reach Europe until 1610. It was around 1860–70 that the 'tea clippers' and their races became famous, competing with one another to be the first home with their precious cargo. Although we are a nation of tea-drinkers, a lot of us still don't make tea really properly. All this and more is in the free packet of information you can get (provided you live in Britain) from: *The Tea Council, 5 High Timber Street, London EC4V 3NJ*

German meats and sausages
If you like delicatessen, the German word for all those tasty products you find in the cooked-meats section of supermarkets, you'll find this glossy sixteen-page booklet fascinating. It provides a guide in colour photographs and text to all kinds of

sausages and other delicacies. 'Wurst' means sausage, 'Rohwurst' are dried or smoked sausages (salami is an example), 'Brühwurst' are the scalded ones (including frankfurters), 'Kochwurst' are the cooked ones such as liver sausage, usually with spices or herbs in them.

This book comes from:

The German Food Centre, 44 Knightsbridge, London SW1

Butter A bright folder called *A Guide to Butter in Britain* (for five- to ten-year-olds) gives lots of interesting facts. Did you know that it takes twenty litres of milk to make one kilo of butter? That Welsh people eat twice as much butter as the English? That the average cow gives over twenty litres of milk each day? The folder has pictures to cut out and two recipes. It also tells you how to make butter yourself, by pouring the cream off the top of the milk and shaking it hard in a screwtop jar for 5–10 minutes (you'll need a lot of energy!) When the fat has separated from the rest of the milk, mix two tablespoons of water into the fat (this will get more milky liquid out of it) and keep shaking until you've got pure butter left. Add a tiny pinch of salt.

If you're interested in a whole sixteen-page booklet on the subject, ask for *The Butter Story* (for elevens and over) which tells you much more about how it is made.

The address to write to for the folder and the booklet is:

The Butter Information Council, The Pantiles House, 2 Nevill Street, Tunbridge Wells, Kent TN2 5TT

Porage and flour The stories of a bag of porage oats and a bag of flour are told in two neat little books with brown and yellow drawings. The Story of Porage begins with an Iron Age caveman grinding his oats, and shows just what's in a single oat grain and what goes on in a modern mill. The flour book gives similar information about wheat from the field to the cake in the oven. Copies are obtainable from:

Rank Hovis McDougall (Consumer Services Dept),
10 Victoria Road, London NW10 6NU

Frozen foods Rather a jolly wall-frieze has been produced by Findus, showing the progress of peas from the field to the kitchen. When you're tired of looking at that, you can turn it over and look at the fish-finger saga or the beef-burger epic instead.

Findus, St George's House, Croydon, Surrey CR9 1NR

Little lamps

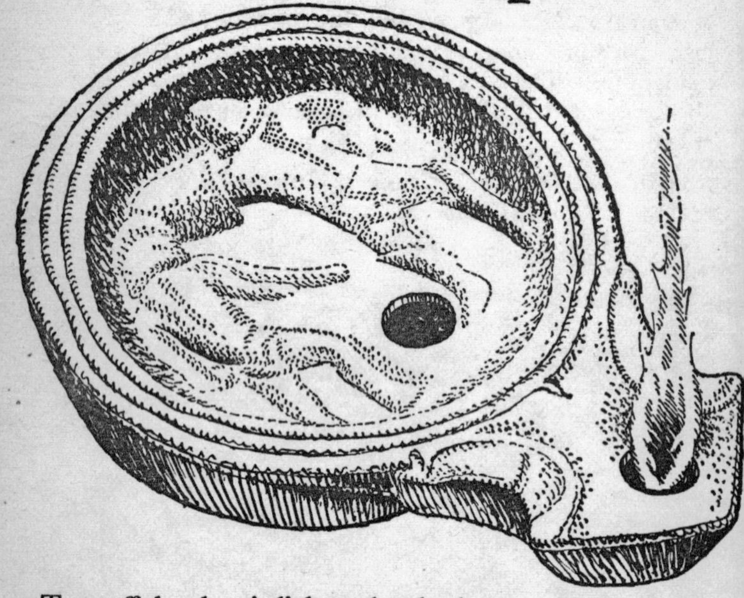

Turn off the electric light and go back a couple of thousand years or so – be a Roman for a while! You'll need the help of an *almost* genuine Roman lamp, moulded exactly to a design of about 200 B.C. and made in reddish pottery very like the Samian ware the Romans used. You can get one by writing to the Tourist Office at Hexham in Northumberland, which is near Hadrian's Wall where lots of things left by the Roman legionaries have been dug up.

Here is a picture of the lamp. This particular design shows two gladiators fighting. You simply put it on its tray, fill it with cooking oil, and light the cotton wick after it has had time to get soaked with oil. A lovely, soft light by which to fall asleep and dream Roman dreams!

folk song and dance

If you're keen on these, you may like to receive the 'Young Folk Bulletin' regularly. It tells you about new records and books, including some to help you learn and play recorder, guitar, etc., and gives details of where you can buy these and other instruments such as dulcimers or pipes. ('Resonant Rubbish' is the title of a £1 book on making musical instruments yourself from waste material. Add 15p postage.)

The Bulletin is free from the English Folk Dance and Song Society. They also have a free catalogue of folk records, but for this send a 10p stamp. Write to:

The Folk Shop, The English Folk Dance and Song Society, Cecil Sharp House, 2 Regent's Park Road, London NW1 7AY

PUZZLING THINGS OUT

If you're a crossword addict and have run out of puzzles to do, send off for a whole book of them. 'Junior Crossword Puzzles', now in its fourteenth edition, has over 120 to keep you busy.

From the same publisher comes a book with seventy brain-teasers of a different kind: picture puzzles.

Don't forget!

1 Write your name and address clearly and say exactly what you want

2 Send the correct money in stamps or postal orders (not cash)

3 Enclose a big enough stamped addressed envelope, if required

4 Address your envelope correctly and stamp it

Where to go, what to do

If you live in or near London, 'Snakes and Ladders' is the guidebook for you. It tells you about conducted tours for young people, ceremonies you can watch, all the museums, what's on in the parks, stacks of places of interest to visit, railways and traction engine rallies, sports, walks, boat trips, cinemas catering specially for young children, and outings to the sea, the country or zoos. Did you know you can phone 01–246 8007 for weekly news of London events for children, and 01–455 6756 for details of summer play centres?

Crystals, 'coppers' and kingfishers

What do these three things have in common? Made in cardboard, they all come from the Natural History Museum in London.

The crystal patterns are drawn on a big sheet waiting to be cut out and formed into cubes, octahedrons, tetrahedrons, zircons, aragonites and the other many-sided shapes in which crystals are found. The Copper is, like the Red Admiral and the Fritillary, a beautiful butterfly – each one presented by the Museum in the form of a greetings card. When you push out the lovely wings of the butterfly, their equally colourful undersides are revealed. As for the Kingfishers, they are just one of several birds the Museum has chosen for make-it-yourself bird mobiles, the others being owls, swallows and merlins. Lots of imaginative ideas here, for showing off the beauties of natural history.

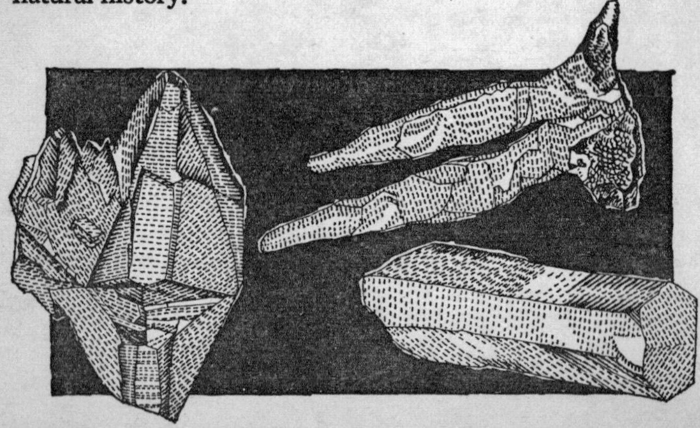

Mexican jumping beans

The real things (not a plastic hoax as sold in some shops) come from a shrub called Yerba de Flecha (meaning 'plant of arrows'), which grows in an exceptionally hot, dry part of Mexico. It gets its name from the fact that its sap was once used by the local Indians to poison the tips of their arrows. Its beans, however, are harmless.

What makes the beans jump ? Thereby hangs another tale. When the plant blossoms, it is visited by the blue-grey Bean Moth, which lays its eggs on the white petals. From these emerge tiny caterpillars which bore into the young bean pods. When the pods are ripe, they suddenly go pop in the heat, scattering the beans inside, some of which the caterpillars will have made into comfortable homes for themselves, lining the walls with the silk they spin.

Now for the strangest part of this long story about a very short bean. The caterpillars keep on making the beans *jump*. Not once or twice, but repeatedly and for many months. Nobody really knows why they do it, but evidently heat is part of the reason, for when you get your jumping beans you need to put them in a warm, light place and leave them undisturbed before they will jump.

Do not order before August or after November.

Are you ever bewildered by the huge number of books in shops and libraries? As you've probably found out, the brightest cover doesn't always go with the best stories.

Here's something to help you choose, and it is interestingly written itself. It's a booklet called 'Reading for Enjoyment', and it comes in four different editions: for 2-5-year-olds, 6-8, 8-11 and 11 up. If you order it, say how old you are.

Each contains information about 200 of the best recent books, both paperback and hardback, fully described and with some pictures.

The booklets come from the Children's Book Centre, which will also supply you by post with any of the books you want from 'Reading for Enjoyment' (and they have 8000 other titles too), if you can't find what you need in your local bookshops.

To keep you up-to-date with news of fresh books as they appear, the Centre also has a quarterly newsletter. They will send you this if you post them £1 – and you get a £1 token to use towards the purchase of any books you then order from them.

Of course, there's nothing to beat browsing round a bookshop and dipping into books before you choose, but ordering by post is the next best thing for those who haven't got a bookshop near home.

good things from Northumbria

Some outstanding posters can be bought from the Northumbria Tourist Board. They're really big, and have first-rate colours. What's your particular interest?

Old steam engines The Stockton & Darlington railway 1825 (the world's first passenger train). This is an extra-big poster; *Dogs* A sheepdog on the Roman Wall; *The American War of Independence* Washington's home and uniform; *Castles* Alnwick, where the English defeated Scots invaders in the 12th century; *Cathedrals* Durham, towering over the river; *History* A picture-map of the ancient kingdom of Northumbria, stretching from Berwick down to Darlington; *The Romans* A spectacular view of Hadrian's Wall; *High Force* A waterfall; *Guisborough Priory* The magnificent east end of the church of the Augustinian Priory; *Tyne Bridges* Sunset view of the Tyne Bridge; *Whitley Bay* View of St Mary's lighthouse.

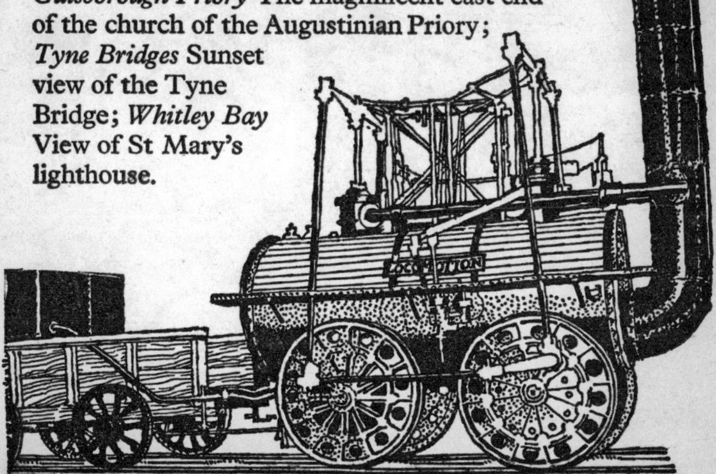

Fellow creatures

Pet-keeping is a wonderful adventure. There are so many interesting things to learn about animals. But it's important to find out before obtaining a pet how to look after it properly. *A Practical Book of Pet-Keeping* is an easy-to-follow guide which is really good value.

If you care about animals, wild or tame, and whether they are safe from cruelty or neglect, you might like to get the badge, membership certificate and magazine of the Crusade against All Cruelty to Animals by joining its Junior Section. Just send your subscription to the Crusade. Your money will help the campaign to end cruelty to animals.

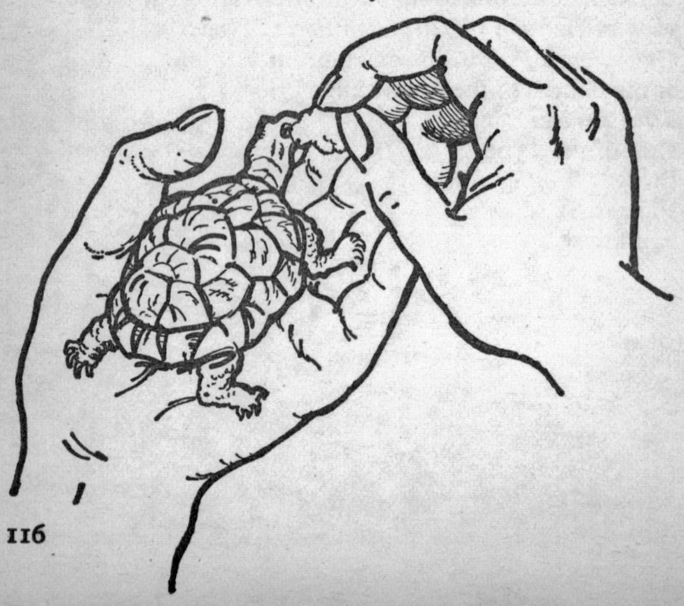

Don't forget!

1 Write your name and address clearly and say exactly what you want

2 Send the correct money in stamps or postal orders (not cash)

3 Enclose a big enough stamped addressed envelope, if required

4 Address your envelope correctly and stamp it

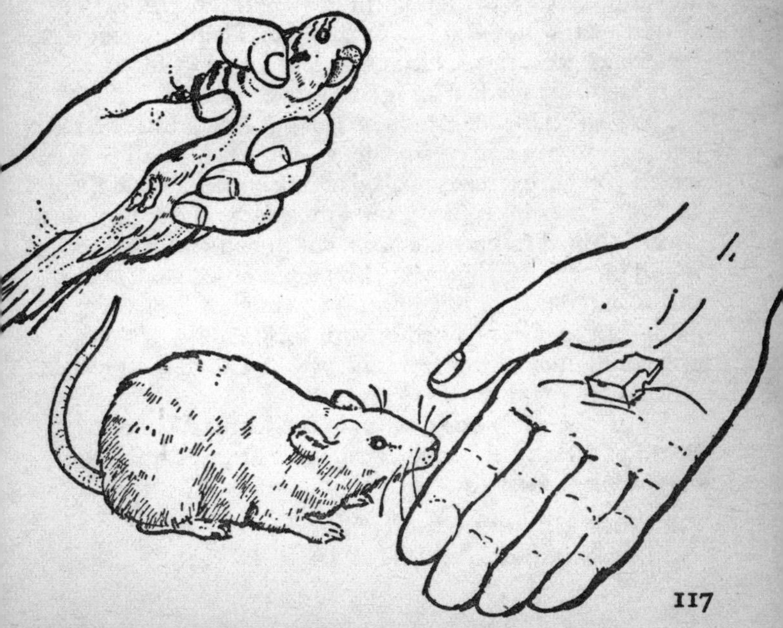

More cookery books

Here are two cookery books that are being given away free – chosen because they include recipes that are easy to do, and because they're nicely printed with good colour pictures.

The Little Orange Party Book is produced by Jaffa. It's full of ideas for party food, games and decorations, and although it's written for mums organising children's parties, you will find it fun to read too. There are recipes for drinks, ices, cakes, biscuits and other party foods, and all of these are made with oranges or grapefruit.

Here's a recipe for a Jaffa hedgehog. Add a little grated orange rind to some cream cheese, and use it to fill prunes, which you have already soaked and de-stoned. Chill the stuffed prunes in the fridge and then spear them on cocktail sticks. Grilled rashers of bacon, cut in half and wrapped round pieces of orange, can also be put on cocktail sticks, and so can pieces of orange wrapped in cheese slices, or grapefruit segments together with cocktail cherries. Stick everything into a grapefruit and you will have an unusual centrepiece for your table!

To get the party book, write to the Citrus Marketing Board of Israel, enclosing a stamped addressed envelope measuring at least 20 × 25 cm.

The Citrus Marketing Board of Israel,
122 Victoria Street, London SW1E 5LA

Sunshine Recipes Sixteen pages of cheese dishes, some quite easy to make, with colour photos, make up this book. Here's a recipe for a 'dip' called Rangitoto Cheese.

Simply stir a packet of leek soup-mix into 3 cartons of soured cream together with 3 dessertspoons of tomato sauce, 75 g grated cheddar and 50 g chopped peanuts. Chill this mixture well before serving. Everyone just dips in with biscuits, crisps, bits of celery or cold chicken-legs – a good idea when you have a lot of your friends in for a meal.

Write for a copy of the book to Anchor Foods Limited. They can also send you 'Have Fun with Anchor Butter', which tells you how to make flavoured butters to serve with different things – like cheesy butter to go on the toast under scrambled egg, mustard butter to go in meat sandwiches, mint butter with lamb, orange butter for pancakes or cinnamon butter for apple pie.

The address to write to is:

Anchor Foods Limited, Bath Road, Swindon, Wilts.

In the frozen North

Do you know how cold it is inside a refrigerator? About 4·5°C. Do you know how cold water is when it turns to ice? 0°C. So imagine what it's like to live in a place where the temperature is *minus* 70°C!

That's Alaska. It's further north than the mainland of Canada, a vast country of ice and snow and very little else – until the day that oil was discovered underground. Now men live there, drilling for the oil and pumping it through great pipes to oil tankers at the coast.

The story of Alaska and its oil is told in a big sixteen-page colouring book; and there is also a kit from which to make a drilling rig if you've got deft fingers for cutting and folding cardboard.

Meet Peter Pelican

If you live in a town, you'll probably find some pelican crossings in the roads, with special lights and a button for you to press. The story of these crossings, and how to make their signals work for you, is told in a kit which you can buy. It consists of a useful plastic wallet containing nine big pictures to stick up round the walls of your room, and a good colouring book with large, clear pictures to paint. The whole thing is called 'The Story of Peter Pelican'.

FREE!

The sporting life

'Sport for All' is the slogan of the Sports Council. To spread the message they will send you, free of charge, a blue-and-white badge with this slogan and their symbol on it (shown here).

Every summer they organise holidays in different parts of England and Wales, where parents and children can go together to enjoy a varied programme of sports – archery, badminton, gym, riding, football, golf, squash, tennis, sailing, trampolining, table tennis, judo, yoga and lots more. Beginners are welcome too. For more details write to:

The Sports Council, 70 Brompton Road, London SW3 1EX

Penfriends for all

FREE!

If you'd like to start up a friendship by post with a boy or girl of about 10–18 living in another country, the 'Links' section of the Central Bureau for Educational Visits and Exchanges will do this for groups or individuals. Write to: *The Central Bureau for Educational Visits and Exchanges, 44 Baker Street, London W1M 2HJ* or *3 Bruntsfield Crescent, Edinburgh EH10 4HD.*

If you want to go it alone, write to one of the following agencies. Give your age, sex and hobbies. This service is free.

Commonwealth:
Commonwealth Friendship Movement,
23 Arundel Road,
Brighton BN2 5TE

U.S.A.:
International Friendship League, Inc.,
22 Batterymarch Street,
Boston,
Massachusetts 02109,
U.S.A.

FREE!

Hurray for the countryside

Alas, England's lovely countryside is in danger, as more and more of it is taken over for buildings. Fortunately, we have the Countryside Commission doing their best to protect what is left. They preserve our great 'national parks' – big areas of open countryside in the north and west, marvellous for holidays or a day's outing. They can send you pictorial leaflets about these if you say what area of the country interests you, and if you like walking, ask for their booklet on recreational paths, or the leaflet on long-distance footpaths and bridleways.

You, too, can help preserve the countryside – it's surprising how much damage is done just through ignorance of the right way to behave in the fields and wild places. The ten rules of 'the Country Code' are: guard against all risk of fire; fasten all gates; keep dogs under proper control; keep to the paths across farm land; avoid damaging fences, hedges and walls; leave no litter; safeguard water supplies; protect wild life, wild plants and trees; go carefully on country roads and respect the life of the countryside.

The rules are explained and illustrated in a very jolly little book which you can ask for, together with a colourful bookmark, leaflet and a bright poster for your room.

All these things come from:

The Countryside Commission, John Dower House, Crescent Place, Cheltenham, Glos. GL50 3RA.

For young cooks

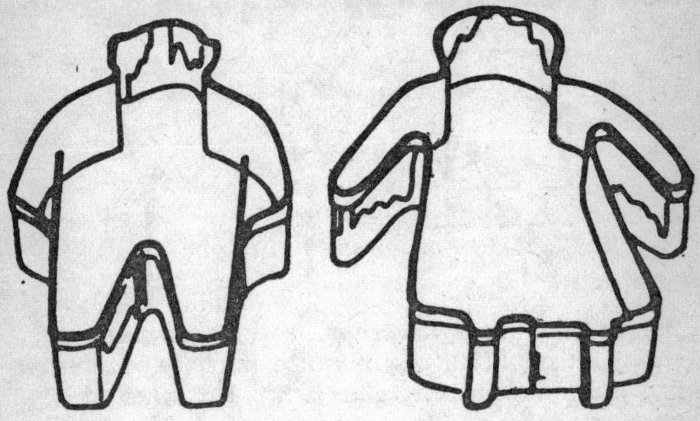

To make gingerbread men you need a special cutter, about 7×15 cm, and you can buy this by post, along with the gingerbread recipe. In fact you can buy cutters for gingerbread women, boys and girls too – and for the Queen, Santa Claus, a snowman and a whole range of farmyard animals. The cutters can also be used to make biscuits.

Gingerbread men, coated in icing, used to be sold at country fairs, but today they have almost vanished. If you try making them yourself, use currants or candied peel to make nose and eyes, or pipe on icing with an icing-tube.

The cutters come from David Mellor, who has a fabulous catalogue illustrating over 700 other things he sells for keen cooks – unusual jelly moulds and cake tins, sweet-making equipment, cake-icing gadgets, butter pats and prints, and much, much more to tempt your mother as well as you into making new goodies in the kitchen.

Tissue paper crafts

What a lot of things you can make with a few sheets of coloured tissue! Collages, of course, but have you thought how pretty a collage on a glass jar will look when varnished? You could even put a candle inside to shine through. You can weave strips of tissue into mats, trim papier mâché models with tissue (including papier mâché beads), plait it to decorate tins or jars or baskets, or make models on wire frameworks. And, of course, there are all sorts of tissue paper flowers.

All these are described in a fascinating little book called 'A Kaleidoscope of Tissue Paper Crafts', written by Yvonne Dockree who also sells complete kits for tissue craft. Each flower kit contains enough coloured tissue paper to make about five sprays of leaves and flowers, plus wires and instructions. These tell you how to make the flowers and how to create a really pretty flower arrangement (designed by the head of the Woburn Abbey School of Flower Arrangement) which will last a very long time if it isn't stood in sunlight or where it may get damp. The flower kits also contain a special flower-assembling platform which makes work easier.

The Harvest-Time kit makes poppies and cornflowers, the Starlight Bouquet contains yellow gladioli and chrysanthemums, Woodland Flowers are pink blossoms and rhododendrons, Special Occasion consists of red roses, lilies and silver filigree on a leather-like platform. If you prefer to make robins and daisies in a silver cage, choose the Tissue Sculpture kit.

An ancient craft

In far-off times, people believed their crops depended on the goodwill of an earth goddess who lived, invisible, in the fields of wheat. When the harvest was gathered in, they saved the best sheaf and made it into a figure – a corn dolly – in which her spirit could live until fresh seeds were sown next spring.

Every country (in fact, every county) had its own way of plaiting and twisting the stalks of wheat into these figures: the Britons first learned the skill when the Romans occupied England. Later, other images began to be made: horns of plenty, love-knots, crosses, horseshoes – all sorts of things associated with good fortune and prosperity.

For a while, the art of making corn dollies was almost forgotten, but now you can not only collect them (some cost under £1) but make your own. The best way to start would be to send for a kit, with instructions, a history of corn dollies, 100 straws to start you off, linen thread and ribbon.

jamjar gardening

If you like nutty flavours, try this. You buy a packet of special seeds (described below). Place some of them in a jar, fix a bit of muslin over the top with a rubber band, fill with water and then, after shaking, drain the water off. Leave the jar on its side with the damp seeds spread out. Wet and drain again every morning and evening, and you will see the seeds growing very rapidly. After 3–6 days (depending on the variety) the seeds and their little shoots will be about eight times bigger and ready to eat. You can use them as they are, in salads or sandwiches, or cook them as a vegetable to serve with meat. They are very nourishing.

Here are some of the different kinds available:

Alfalfa (tastes like baby peas), Fenugreek (a bit spicy), Adzuki (crisp and nutty), Chinese bamboo bean shoots, Sparkling Lentil (nutty and a bit sweet), Alphatoco (crisp), Soya Bean (nutty).

You can buy a mixture of seeds in a packet of Salad Sprouts or Saucy Sandwich Relish, if you prefer.

the holy land

You can get a huge map of Israel with little pictures showing where all the famous historical sites are – places like Jerusalem, Bethlehem, Nazareth and so on. On the back, more information is given about each of them – and about orange- and grapefruit-growing in Israel, for the map is given away by the Jaffa citrus-growers. Send a stamped addressed envelope at least 25 × 30 cm to:

The Citrus Marketing Board of Israel, 122 Victoria Street, London SW1E 5LA.

Don't forget!

1. Write your name and address clearly and say exactly what you want
2. Send the correct money in stamps or postal orders (not cash)
3. Enclose a big enough stamped addressed envelope, if required
4. Address your envelope correctly and stamp it

Poly crafts

Poly crafts are things you make with Polycell paste or Polyfilla (a plaster-like material), both sold by hardware or home-decorating shops. The makers of these products have produced two sets of cards telling you how to make a whole lot of things. The cards are big (15 × 20 cm) and glossy (you can wipe them clean if they get messy), with beautiful clear drawings of what to do, and really brilliant colours. Each set of fourteen comes in a plastic wallet.

Set A (yellow) tells you how to make beads, bookends, finger-printed patterns, a papier mâché owl, eggshell collage, animal models, patterned inlay tiles, paperweights, eggshell-mould people, a paper-strip dinosaur, a snowman from junk, a textured cottage, a helter-skelter for your miniature cars and a robot collage.

Set B (red) has instructions for making arm puppets, a carved totem-pole, textured tiles, seed collage, a modelled starfish, an astronauts' moon base, decorated pots, stiffened bag-masks, inlay patterns, a model village, a cloth-sculpture witch, a dragon from junk, a silvery tree and a castle.

If you get really carried away with these new hobbies, you might like to have 'Polytechniques' – a folder containing twenty wallsheets (each over 60 cm long) telling you of lots more methods you can use creatively. These include piped Polyfilla, fabric-stiffening, sawdust modelling, appliqué, plastic glazing, papier mâché, no-wax batik, scraperboard pictures, paper basketry, inlay, relief panels, gesso, print transfers, salt modelling, play dough, découpage, shell and pasta decorations, cloth sculpture, plaster carving and many other ideas.

After school– what?

If you're beginning to wonder what sort of work you'd like to do when you finish your education, *The Job Quiz Books* (there are three of them) are for you. Though there's a good deal of food for thought in them, there are lots of lighter touches too – like this teaser on famous people, each of whom began his or her career as something quite different from their present work. Can you fit the original occupations to the names of the men or women?

1	Mao Tse Tung	a	shop assistant
2	Enoch Powell	b	gravedigger
3	Max Bygraves	c	preacher
4	Twiggy	d	storekeeper
5	Abraham Lincoln	e	assistant librarian
6	Rod Stewart	f	professor of Greek
7	Mike Yarwood	g	painter and decorator
8	Oliver Hardy	h	boxer
9	Idi Amin	i	lumberjack
10	Casanova	j	law student

Answers:
1 (e), 2 (f), 3 (g), 4 (a), 5 (i), 6 (b), 7 (d), 8 (j), 9 (h), 10 (c).

The Red Cross to the rescue

Wherever there is disaster, the Red Cross workers are to be found – nursing, feeding and comforting. The Youth and Junior section helps too. War, floods, famine, missing people, accidents – the Red Cross can always be relied upon to help. A Swiss man began it all back in 1863, but now 200 million people help in its work.

A very big, coloured wallchart tells the Red Cross story, and there is a free leaflet too (send 15p in stamps for postage). Why not ask about joining the Junior section too? The address is:

British Red Cross Society, Youth and Juniors Department, 9 Grosvenor Crescent, London SW1X 7EJ

Money matters

Perhaps the nicest money-box for your savings is a china cottage, which you can get from the Museum of Childhood in Wales. Maybe you'd also like their booklet of delicious little toys like the one below, photographed in colour – funny old money-boxes, Victorian doll's furniture, old toy trains, clockwork vintage cars, antique dolls and so forth.

Other unusual money-boxes are sold by banks. There's no need to order these by post – just call at a local branch and ask to be shown one. The National Westminster Bank has a very attractive one in the shape of a blue-and-gold globe showing all the countries of the world. It's transparent (so you can see what you've got inside) and has a key.

Catalogues for kids

If there's a particular kind of toy, game or hobby you're keen on, you can usually send off for a complete catalogue to browse through in order to build up your collection. In America, such tempting catalogues are aptly called 'wish books'! Here are a few examples.

ACTION MAN Palitoy, Coalville, Leicester
CORGI Mettoy Playcraft Ltd, 14 Harlestone Road, Northampton
CRAFTS, ALL KINDS Materials and books. Fred Aldous Ltd, 37 Lever Street, Manchester M60 1UX
ENAMELLING, PLASTIC CASTING Turner Research Ltd, Jubilee Terrace, Leeds LS6 2XH
LEGO British Lego Ltd, Wrexham LL13 9UH
PAPER THINGS Everything under the sun. Paperchase, 216 Tottenham Court Road, London W1
PLAYPEOPLE Louis Marx Ltd, Industrial Estate, Swansea
TOYS FOR ALL AGES Hamleys, Regent Street, London W1R 6BT
TOYS FOR YOUNG CHILDREN:
Abbatts, Pinnacles, Harlow, Essex;
John Adams, Crazies Hill, Wargrave, Berks;
Bagatelle, 7 Gun Street, Reading, Berks;
Beaver (wooden toys), Marlborough, Wilts;
Galts, Cheadle, Cheshire

Index and Further Information

After school, what? (page 131) First two books 55p, third book 65p. Plus 30p postage from Hobsons Press, Bateman Street, Cambridge CB2 1LZ. Ask for their free catalogue
All about dinosaurs (page 16) Models: Megalosaurus 65p, Diplodocus £1.95, Scelidosaurus 20p, Triceratops £1.10, Stegosaurus 63p, Tyrannosaurus Rex £1.35 (set of six £5.35); Pteranodon 50p, Plesiosaur £1.35. Posters 30p each. Colour postcards £1 a set, black-and-white 2p each. Badges 10p. Wallchart £1.10. Wall plaque 45p. Book 75p. Add 10% postage (minimum 30p) to each order, except for postcards (add 8p for up to 5) and badges (add 10p). All from Publications (Sales), Natural History Museum, Cromwell Road, London SW7 5BD. Coloured postacrds in pack 8 for 50p plus 20p postage and a stamped envelope at least 10 × 15 cm from The Publications Unit, Birmingham Museums and Art Gallery, Chamberlain Square, Birmingham B3 3DH
Along the Clipper Way (page 60) £1.90 plus 40p postage from Francis Chichester Ltd, 9 St James's Place, London SW1A 1PE
An ancient craft (page 127) £1.85 from Felcraft, 15 Ludlow Avenue, North Shields NE29 9EY
Are you a dog-lover? (page 73) Dog chart 35p plus 15p postage from National Canine Defence League, 10 Seymour Street, London W1
Art for the bone-idle (page 99) individual stamps cost between 20p and 35p, and the ink-pad costs 69p. Send a s.a.e. for details to: Andover Rubber Stamp Service, Balksbury Farm, Upper Clatford SP11 7LW
The best stories (page 114) 40p each including postage from Children's Book Centre, Little Mead, Alfold Road, Cranleigh, Surrey GU6 8NU
British uniforms (page 64) 5p each plus postage (12p for up to ten colouring sheets). From National Army Museum, Royal Hospital Road, London SW3 4HT
Buried treasure! (page 48) Maps 60p, posters 54p. Plus 8p postage in each case. From Porter Prints, 16 Stonegate, York
By Golly! (page 70) Aprons £1.40 (adult size £1.95), bag £1.95, doll £3.95, stretch baseball cap £1.10, beanie hat £1.10 (or large £1.30), belt 60p, T-shirts (state your age and chest size) £1.10. Send 2 paper Gollies from jars of jam etc. for each item. From J. Robertson & Sons P. M. Ltd, Golden Shred Works, Droylsden, Manchester M35 6DR
Canals are having a comeback (page 24) Posters 55p plus 35p postage (or 70p for 2 or more) from Canal Shop and Information Centre, British Waterways Board, Melbury House, Melbury

Terrace, London NW1 6JX; 'Canals are Great' 50p plus 15p postage; 'Fun on the Waterways' 65p plus 20p postage; 'The Story of our Canals' 40p plus 15p postage. 32p for postage if you buy all three books.

Cardboard dolls (page 33) From Museum of Costume, Assembly Rooms, Bath: 10p each plus 20p postage for one or a set of three. From Royal Scottish Museum, Edinburgh EH1 1JF: 8p plus 10p postage (send cheque or postal order for 18p)

Catalogues for kids (page 134)

Chess by post (page 56)

The Choice is Ours (page 97) 60p each from Society for the Promotion of Nature Conservation, The Green, Nettleham, Lincoln LN2 2NR

City wildlife (page 75) Book 40p including postage, record 64p including postage. From Humane Education Centre, Avenue Lodge, Bounds Green Road, London N22 4EU

Coins and their history (page 38)

Country parks (page 55)

Countryside posters (page 86) Pop posters 4 for £1.20 (40p each), charts 5 for £3.00. Prices include postage. From Council for the Protection of Rural England, 4 Hobart Place, London SW1W 0HY

Creatures great and small (page 34) Leaflets 5p each from Publications (Sales), Natural History Museum, Cromwell Road, London SW7 5BD

Crystals, 'Coppers' and kingfishers (page 112) Crystal models: 2 sheets 10p each plus 20p postage for either or both. Butterfly greetings cards 32p each post free (12 cards in all). Bird mobiles: swallow or kingfisher £1.20, owl £1.40, merlin £1.50, set of four £5 – plus 25p postage for one or more. From Publications (Sales), Natural History Museum, Cromwell Road, London SW7 5BD

Down on the farm (page 89)

Embroidery know-how (page 20) '100 Embroidery Stitches' 40p, '50 Free-Style Embroidery Stitches' 75p, plus 15p postage in each case. From Royal School of Needlework Shop, 25 Princes Gate, London SW7 1QE

Famous faces (page 88) Colouring book 40p plus 25p postage from National Portrait Gallery, Publications Dept, 2 St Martins Place, London WC2 0HE

Fellow creatures (page 116) Pet book 60p including postage from Crusade Against All Cruelty to Animals, Humane Education Centre, Avenue Lodge, Bounds Green Road, London N22 4EU. Subscription 40p to Junior Section, same address

Finding out what's where (page 10) Aircraft in Action, Birds of Britain, Coins of Western Europe, Football, *Golden Hinde*, Historical North England, Horse & Pony, Lifeboats, Passenger Trains, Postal History, Railway History, Royal Ancestors, Royal Scotland,

Scientists & Inventors, Tartans, Vintage Cars, World of Animals, Flowers, Insects, Flight (2 maps), Sail, Stamps, Vanishing Flowers – all 95p each including postage. Armada, Bonnie Prince Charlie – 25p each including postage. From John Bartholomew Ltd, Duncan Street, Edinburgh

Flying high (page 7) War kite size 4, £3.86; Hawk kite size 3, £8.20. Plus 25p postage in each case. From Brookite Ltd, Francis Terrace Mews, London N19 5PY

Folk song and dance (page 109)

Foot games (page 12)

For busy bees (page 35) From the National Federation of Women's Institutes, 39 Eccleston Street, London SW1. 'Basic Macramé', 'Collage and Fabric Pictures', 'Embroidered Boxes', 'Hedgerow Baskets', 'Paper Sculpture' – 15p each. 'Knitting for Beginners', 20p. 'Broomstick Crochet' and 'Log Cabin Patchwork' 25p each. 'Simple Wood Sculpture' 30p. 'Soft Toys Galore' 50p. 'Bits for Bazaars' 75p. Add 12p for orders up to 20p in value, 24p for orders of 25–50p and 32p for orders over 50p.

For ship enthusiasts (page 84) £1.50 each including postage from The Marine Society, 202 Lambeth Road, London SE1 7JW

45,000,000 years ago (page 95) Oligocene chart 65p, portions of turtle 15p and crocodile 20p–85p according to size. Prices include postage but exclude VAT at 15% extra. From Watkins & Doncaster, Four Throws, Hawkhurst, Kent

For young cooks (page 125) Cutters: men 75p, women 76p, queen 59p, small boys and girls 39p, Father Christmas 59p; Snowman £1.99; 12 small farm animals £4.95. Plust 30p postage and (if your order is above £1) a further 8p for each additional £1 of goods. From David Mellow, 4 Sloane Square, London SW1

For young zoologists (page 43) Catalogue 50p; list history of ladybird, £2.20, butterfly £2.20, locust £2.40; fircones 8 for £2.45, 15 for £3.75; insect prints 60p each; large charts: butterflies 70p, others 80p; sets of small charts: birds (2 sets of 4), fish (4), trees (4), all 70p a set; mammals (6) 80p; breeding cage for insects 80p; beginner's butterfly net £1.95. All prices include postage but exclude VAT at 15% extra. From Watkins & Doncaster, Four Throws, Hawkhurst, Kent

Fred Basset's on the scent (page 74) Strip cartoon books 50p each plus 12p postage. From Publications Department, Associated Newspapers Group Ltd, Carmelite House, London EC4Y 0JA

Fun with colour (page 45) Dylon leaflets from Dylon International Ltd, Lower Sydenham, London SE26 5HD. Tie-and-dye kit £1.25 plus 85p postage; Colour-fun Fabric Painting Kit £2.95 plus 85p postage; transfer packs 40p each plus a self-addressed envelope measuring at least 13 × 20 cm; all from Crownwell Ltd, 11 Market Street, Watford, Herts WD1 7AA

Get glueing! (page 69) 35p plus 10p postage from Gloy, Eighth Avenue, London E12 5JW
Getting in the swim (page 23)
Good things from Northumbria (page 115) Stockton rail poster 75p plus 15p postage, others 60p plus 15p postage. From Northumbria Tourist Board, Newcastle-upon-Tyne
The greatest story in the world (page 90) 'Jesus and His Message of Liberation' £1.50 (plus 15p postage unless ordered through a bookshop), 'Compass' 45p per issue or £1.25 a year (check price first if you write after 1979). From Bible Reading Fellowship, 2 Elizabeth Street, London SW1W 9RQ
A guide to garden birds (page 25)
'Hands Off These Animals!' (page 93) Poster 57p including postage. From Council for Nature, Zoological Gardens, London NW1 4RY
Have you got 'green fingers'? (page 32) Vegetable or flower collections 50p each, mustard and cress farm 60p, mung beans 40p. Add 25p postage if your order totals less than £3.50. From Suttons Seeds Ltd, Torquay, Devon
Historical costume (page 52) 'Fashion Designs of the 1830s' 55p plus 20p postage, 'Fashion Outlines' 7p each. Postage 12p. From Museum of Costume, Assembly Rooms, Bath
Holidays with a difference (page 11) 'Activity and Hobby Holidays in England '79' 50p plus 15p postage. From Activity Holidays '79, Hendon Road, Sunderland SR9 9XZ.
The Holy Land (page 129)
How it used to be (page 83) £1.95 each including postage from David & Charles, Newton Abbot, Devon. Send for full details of maps available
How to make posters (page 21) Screen-printing leaflet 10p including postage from National Association of Youth Clubs, Blackburn House, Bond Gate, Nuneaton, Warwickshire
Hurray for the countryside (page 124)
If you're keen on sewing . . . (page 41) £2.85 each from Education Department, English Sewing Ltd, 56 Oxford Street, Manchester M60 1HJ
Industry at work (page 80) Cut-out models 70p from BP Education Service, P.O. Box 5, Wetherby, West Yorkshire LS23 7EH. 'Blue Circle Cement' from The Blue Circle Group (Publicity Dept), Portland House, Stag Place, London SW1E 5BJ
In the frozen North (page 120) 'Alaskan Adventure' colouring book 50p; drilling-rig model 92p. BP Education Service, Britannic House, Moor Lane, London EC2Y 9BU
Introducing Effie (page 71)
Is it a money-box? (page 62) £1 including postage (3 for £2.70) from Holt & Park, 8 Athelstan Road, Bitterne, Southampton

Jamjar gardening (page 128) Send a stamped addressed envelope for current prices (most seeds are 60–70p a packet). From Thompson & Morgan, Crane Hall, Ipswich IP2 0BA
Karoline the Kow (page 59)
'Keep Britain Tidy' (page 39) Colour posters 40p (small ones 25p); T-shirts: white £1.75, yellow £1.50, plus 50p postage. From Keep Britain Tidy Group, 37 West Street, Brighton BN1 2RE
Little lamps (page 108) £2.20 plus 30p postage. Includes lamp, old fashioned tray, wick and presentation box. From Tourist Information Centre, Manor Office, Hallgates, Hexham, Northumberland
London life in bygone times (page 22) 'Little Fanny' 99p plus 10p postage; board games 85p each plus 10p postage; poster 40p plus 10p postage; tins £1.45 plus 20p postage. From the London Museum Shop, London Wall, London EC2Y 5HN
London's Transport (page 57)
Make or break (page 29) £3.99 including postage from The Sylglas Co., Denso House, Chapel Road, West Norwood, London SE27
Make your own candles (page 98) For prices and a complete list of products, write to this address, enclosing a s.a.e.: Candle Makers Supplies, 28 Blythe Road, London W14 0HA
Making music (page 26) Small (high-pitch) £2, medium £2.50, large (low-pitch) £3 (prices include postage). From Gangadar, The Laurels, School Lane, East Harling, Norfolk
Making toys (page 92) 'Do It Yourself' 70p, 'Design and Make Magnetic Board Toys' 50p. Prices include postage. From Toy Libraries Association, Seabrook Ho., Wyllyotts Manor, Darkes Lane, Potters Bar, Herts EN6 2HL
A medieval touch (page 37) Coin rings 40p each, pendants £2.25, hare brooch £1.25. Plus 15p postage in each case. From Salisbury Museum Replicas Ltd, 40 St Ann Street, Salisbury, Wilts
Meet Peter Pelican (page 121) £1.90 from BP Education Service, Britannic House, Moor Lane, London EC2Y 9BU
Men of the sea (page 54) Cross-section of ship 25p, wallcharts 55p. Both prices include postage. From The Marine Society, 202 Lambeth Road, London SE1 7JW
Mexican jumping beans (page 113) 5 beans in container with leaflet 50p including postage from Uropets, 37B Mildmay Grove, London N1 4RH
Money matters (page 133) Money box £4, booklet 50p. Both prices include postage. From Museum of Childhood, Water Street, Menai Bridge, Anglesey
More cookery books (page 118)
More pet-care leaflets (page 91) Subscription 25p; *Busy Bees News* 90p a year; *Guild News* is free. From PDSA, South Street, Dorking, Surrey

Neptune in colour (page 65) Neptune 55p, coin rings 60p, coin sets £2.40. From Corinium Museum, Park Street, Cirencester, Glos. GL7 2BX

New hobbies (page 9) Paper-maker kit £6.46, Fabric collage £3.69 (say whether you prefer owl or elephant design), Papier-mâché £1.84, New-clay set £2.77, 'Fun with Art' £1.99. Plus 15% VAT on all items. Orders over £8 post free, otherwise £1.40 per order. From James Galt & Co. Ltd, Brookfield Road, Cheadle, Cheshire

Old transport (page 68) 'Lion' and 'Hope' 22p each plus 30p postage, balloon map of Liverpool 38p, prints: 'The Landing Stage 1880' 35p, 'Railway Scene' 18p. Postage on one or all of these 20p. From Merseyside County Museums, William Brown Street, Liverpool L3 8EN

Other people's lives (page 61)

Outings in London (page 102)

P is for pasta (page 27) Wallchart 25p from Pasta Information Centre, 26 Fitzroy Square, London W1P 6BT

Paper capers (page 78)

Penfriends for all (page 123)

Pets galore (page 51) Send your enrolment fee of 15p to National Pets Club, Athene House, 66/73 Shoe Lane, London EC4P 4AB

Pick of the posters (page 79) £1.35. Postage 80p for one or more. From London Transport Shop, 280 Old Marylebone Road, London NW1 5RJ

Planning a party? (page 50) Send a £1 deposit (returnable) plus 25p postage to Barnums, 67 Hammersmith Road, London W14 8UY

Poly crafts (page 130) Craft cards (yellow or red) 50p per set, 'Polytechniques' £1. From Polycell, Broadwater Road, Welwyn Garden City AL7 3AZ

A pond in your room (page 28) £1.50 including postage from Fords of Bristol Ltd, Tower House, Fairfax Street, Bristol BS1 3BS

Posters unlimited (page 63) 'Child Education Special' costs 45p per issue, £3.60 a year, and can be ordered from any newsagent. If ordered from the publisher (Evans, Montague House, Russell Square, London WC1B 5BX) it is 61p per copy including postage

Pottery at home (page 76) 5 kg bag of clay £3.60 including postage; 350 g jar of ColdGlaze £2.57; work cards 32 for £3.50. From Fulham Pottery, 210 New Kings Road, London SW6 4NY

Pretty plants – with a warning (page 36) 25p plus 12p postage from Mother & Baby Advice Pamphlets, M. & A. P. Ltd, P.O. Box 35, Bridge Street, Hemel Hempstead, Herts HP1 1EE

Puzzling things out (page 110) 'Junior Crossword Puzzles' 45p plus 10p postage; 'Picture Puzzles' 35p plus 8p postage.Both from Publications Department, Associated Newspapers Group Ltd, Carmelite House, London EC4Y 0JA

The real Red Indians (page 15) £1.50 each plus 30p postage from Edward Patterson Associates Ltd, 68 Copers Cope Road, Beckenham, Kent
The Red Cross to the rescue (page 132)
The Roman Wall (page 17) Poster map 50p plus 20p postage. From Hexham Tourist Information Centre, Manor Office, Hallgates, Hexham, Northumberland
Save These Flowers (page 58) 50p including postage from Botanical Society of the British Isles Publications, Oundle Lodge, Oundle PE8 5TN
Scotland for children (page 44) 50p each including postage from Scottish Tourist Board, 23 Ravelston Terrace, Edinburgh EH4 3EU
Seven games at a go (page 94) Single £3.95 plus 40p postage, double £6.45 plus 70p postage. From Clothkits, 24 High Street, Lewes BN7 2LU. Say whether you prefer red or blue background
Sheep-spotter's guide (page 72) Poster £1, 'British Sheep Breeds' book £1.90, 'Three Bags Full' 65p. From Promotion Department, British Wool Marketing Board, Oak Mills, Station Road, Clayton, Bradford BD14 6JD
Sizzling sausages (page 49)
Something fishy (page 96) Send a s.a.e. to White Fish Kitchen, 30 Farringdon Street, London EC4A 4EA
Something for eggheads (page 30)
Something to paint (page 42) 35p each plus 20p postage from Publications (Sales), Natural History Museum, Cromwell Road, London SW7 5BD
The sporting life (page 122)
S.S. *Great Britain* (page 100) Souvenir Shop, S.S. *Great Britain*, The Docks, Bristol. 50p each plus 67p postage in a strong tube from National Maritime Museum, Greenwich, London SE10 9NF
Star gymnasts (page 53) 'World Star Gymnasts' 60p, posters of individual stars £1 (or 4 for £3); 8 postcards 80p. All prices include postage. From Jaffa Gym Fund, c/o Hendon Sports Centre, Algernon Road, London NW4 3TA
Sweet treats (page 87) Cookcards 95p including postage from British Sugar Bureau, 140 Park Lane, London W1Y 3AA
'There she blows!' (page 77) £1.10 plus 40p postage from Francis Chichester Ltd, 9 St James's Place, London SW1A 1PE
A tiger, an elephant and a rabbit (page 85) Posters 86p for 3, 'party' kit £1.44. From General Dental Council, 37 Wimpole Street, London W1M 8DQ
Time to wash (page 81)
Tin whistle (page 96) £4.50 plus 35p postage. Say whether you want a record or a cassette. Appletree Press, 6 Dublin Road, Belfast BT2 7HL

Tissue paper crafts (page 126) 'Kaleidoscope' 50p; flower kits £1.20 or 2 for £1.90; sculpture kit 70p. All prices include postage. From Yvonne Docktree, 28 Mile House Lane, St Albans AL1 1TB

Toy theatres – plus plus plus! (page 46) Theatres with actors etc. for 'Ali Baba' £1.20, for 'Cinerella' £1.30, plus 35p postage. Ask for free list of other plays. 'How to dress an old-fashioned doll' £1 plus 15p postage, cut-and-sew puppets 40p each plus 15p postage, scrapbook £1.35 plus 35p postage and sheets of scraps 12p, rag dolls and cat £1.60 each plus 15p postage, blank jig-saw £1.30, doll's house wallpapers 20p a sheet (51 × 71 cm – state required colour) plus 20p postage, books of colour-and-cut dolls £1.50 each plus 35p postage, Victorian parlour £1.20 plus 35p postage. From Pollocks, 1 Scala Street, London W1

Trams, trains and trinkets (page 8) Tram cut-out 40p plus 12½p postage, jigsaw 40p plus 9p postage, miner's lamp necklace £1.20, plus 9p postage, book about Beamish 30p plus 9p postage. Beamish Hall, County Durham

A trip to the theatre (page 19)

Wales is wonderful (page 40)

Where to go, what to do (page 111) 'Snakes and Ladders' 60p including postage from Westminster Play Association, 16/18Strutton Ground, London SW1

Who's afraid of the big, bad exam? (page 18) Model answers 90p each from Artemis Press, Sedgwick Park, Horsham, Sussex; 'Your Choice at 13+' £1.10 plus 30p postage from Hobsons Press, Bateman Street, Cambridge CB2 1LZ

Wildlife posters (page 13) Posters: Plants £1 each, Chi-Chi 10p, Butterflies £1; prints: £1. Plus 10% postage (minimum 30p). From Publications (Sales), Natural History Museum, Cromwell Road, London SW7 5BD

Wild places in your world (page 31) Lowland Farmland, Sand Dunes, Salt Marshes and Last Glaciation wallcharts 65p each. All available, together with leaflets and details of other publications from The Library, Nature Conservancy Council, 19/20 Belgrave Square, London SW1X 8PY

World families (page 66) £1.50 the set plus 12p VAT from Centre for World Development Education, 128 Buckingham Palace Road, London SW1

Young Rescue (page 82)

Young volunteers (page 14) Send 15p and an envelope measuring at least 25 × 33 cm to National Youth Bureau, 17 Albion Street, Leicester LE1 8PY

Your camera (page 67)

Your favourite foods (page 103)

We hope you have enjoyed this Beaver Book. Here are some of the other titles:

All Your Own A Beaver original. Hundreds of ideas for transforming all – or part – of an ordinary bedroom into an exciting place to suit all your needs. Written by Elizabeth Gundrey and illustrated by Virginia Smith

Crazy Crosswords A Beaver original. Gyles Brandreth has devised, and Rowan Barnes Murphy has drawn, forty crazy crosswords for fans of all ages. Some have word clues, some picture clues and some give you the answers before you start! Another fun-filled book from the author of *Be Kind to Mum and Dad*, also published by Beavers

True Adventures of the Wild West A Beaver original. Eighteen stories of the wild west, from Custer's Last Stand to the Alamo and the short-lived venture of the Pony Express, told by Robin May and illustrated by Harry Bishop

Paper Fun A Beaver original. Eric Kenneway shows you how easily paper can be made into all sorts of games, toys and decorations, from a frisbee to a telephone or a blowpipe and darts. Step-by-step diagrams and amusing illustrations by Alan Rogers accompany the text

These and many other Beavers are available at your local bookshop or newsagent, or can be ordered direct from: Hamlyn Paperback Cash Sales, PO Box 11, Falmouth, Cornwall TR10 9EN. Send a cheque or postal order, made payable to The Hamlyn Publishing Group, for the price of the book plus postage at the following rates:
UK: 22p for the first book plus 10p a copy for each extra book ordered to a maximum of 92p;
BFPO and EIRE: 22p for the first book plus 10p a copy for the next 6 books and thereafter 4p a book;
OVERSEAS: 30p for the first book and 10p for each extra book.

New Beavers are published every month and if you would like the *Beaver Bulletin*, which gives a complete list of books and prices, including new titles, send a large stamped addressed envelope to:

Beaver Bulletin
The Hamlyn Group
Astronaut House
Feltham
Middlesex TW14 9AR

200388